WHAT ENCOURAGES GANG BEHAVIOR?

Other books in the At Issue series:

Affirmative Action
Animal Experimentation
Anti-Semitism
The Attacks on America: September 11, 2001
Child Labor and Sweatshops
Child Sexual Abuse
Cloning
Creationism vs. Evolution
Date Rape
Does Capital Punishment Deter Crime?
Drunk Driving
The Ethics of Euthanasia
Ethnic Conflict
Food Safety
The Future of the Internet
Gay Marriage
Guns and Crime
How Can Gun Violence Be Reduced?
Human Embryo Research
Immigration Policy
Interracial Relationships
Is Media Violence a Problem?
Legalizing Drugs
Marijuana
The Media and Politics
Physician-Assisted Suicide
Professional Wrestling
Rain Forests
Rape on Campus
Satanism
School Shootings
Sex Education
Sexually Transmitted Diseases
Single-Parent Families
Smoking
The Spread of AIDS
Teen Sex
Teen Suicide
UFOs
The United Nations
U.S. Policy Toward China
Violent Children
Voting Behavior
Welfare Reform
What Is a Hate Crime?

WHAT ENCOURAGES GANG BEHAVIOR?

Tamara L. Roleff, *Book Editor*

Daniel Leone, *President*
Bonnie Szumski, *Publisher*
Scott Barbour, *Managing Editor*

An Opposing Viewpoints® Series

Greenhaven Press, Inc.
San Diego, California

Library of Congress Cataloging-in-Publication Data

What encourages gang behavior? / Tamara L. Roleff, book editor.
    p. cm. — (At issue)
    Includes bibliographical references and index.
    ISBN 0-7377-0810-7 (pbk. : alk. paper) —
ISBN 0-7377-0811-5 (lib. : alk. paper)
    1. Gangs. 2. Gang members—Psychology. I. Roleff, Tamara L.,
1959– II. At issue (San Diego, Calif.)

HV6437 .W48   2002
364.1'06'6019—dc21   2001040745
                                                    CIP

Contents

Introduction

From the time they are very young, most children and adolescents play and socialize with friends they meet in various places—their neighborhood, school, church, scouts, sports and other hobbies, and at work. Most of these groups offer positive experiences for children because they fulfill their emotional needs for friends and acceptance, give them structure and support in their lives, and teach them valuable skills such as how to get along with others. Some children, however, associate with groups that are more antisocial in nature—gangs.

There is no one standard definition of what constitutes a gang, but generally, researchers agree with Sandra Gardner's definition of a gang:

> An organization of young people usually between their early teens and early twenties, which has a group name, claims a territory or neighborhood as its own, meets with its members on a regular basis, and has recognizable leadership.

To further distinguish themselves as gangs, most gang members dress in one particular color associated with their gang, have gang symbols tattooed on themselves, and use graffiti to mark their territory and to send messages to rival gangs. But "the key element that distinguishes a gang from other organizations of young people," Gardner adds, "is delinquency: its members regularly participate in activities that violate the law."

Studies have found that gang members commit serious and violent crime at a higher rate than teens who are not members of gangs. A 1996 study estimated that nearly 600,000 crimes in the United States were committed by gang members in 1993. Researchers in Denver, Seattle, and Rochester, New York, reported that teen gang members committed more than three, five, and seven times, respectively, as many violent crimes than nongang adolescents. In addition, most gang members own a gun, many of them illegally. The increasing number of guns and their use by gang members is linked to a rise in gang-related homicides. Law enforcement officials in Los Angeles determined that the proportion of gang-related homicides involving guns increased from 71 percent in 1979 to 95 percent in 1994.

Although the main activity of gang members is hanging out, drinking, using drugs, and going to parties or concerts together, delinquent and criminal activities are often the focus of gang culture. Motivated by thrills, excitement, and the potential to make money, many gang members shoplift, mug innocent passers-by, steal cars, use and sell drugs, and plan and participate in gangbangs—fights—with rival gangs. Billy, a twenty-one-year-old Crip gang member, tells Scott H. Decker and Barrik Van Winkle in *Life in the Gang* how he and his fellow gang members spend a typical day:

Do different things just like a family. Hang out together, rob, steal cars, fight other gangs like for competition. Mostly just fight against other gang members.

The number of gangs has proliferated in the United States since 1980. The Office of Juvenile Justice and Delinquency Prevention reports that the number of counties, towns, and cities with gangs increased from 286 in 1980 with 2,000 gangs and 100,000 members to 4,463 localities in 1998 with 28,700 gangs and 780,200 members. The National Youth Gang Center surveyed just over 3,000 law enforcement agencies in the United States and found that 48 percent of police and sheriff's departments reported that youth gangs were active in their area in 1998. No state is immune from gangs and neither are small towns; half of all law enforcement agencies reporting gang activity are in areas with a population under 25,000. Surveys have shown that between 14 percent and 30 percent of adolescents and young adults in urban areas—usually between the ages of twelve and twenty-four—join gangs.

At first, most gangs were observed in poverty-stricken, inner-city neighborhoods, leading some researchers to believe that a depressed economy encouraged youth to join gangs because there were so few job opportunities for them. However, in the 1980s and 1990s, gangs began emerging in affluent suburbs and experts began to change their theories about why teens joined gangs. Dan Korem, author of *Suburban Gangs: The Affluent Rebels*, found that nearly every gang member he studied over seven years—in both affluent and lower-income neighborhoods in the United States and Europe—had one trait in common. According to Korem, *"Every youth in each of the gangs came from a broken, unstable, or severely dysfunctional home"* (emphasis in original). The parents of each gang member he observed were either divorced or separated, or the parents were severely dysfunctional, such as an alcoholic or mentally ill, or one or more family members were victims of physical, sexual, or emotional abuse in the home.

When adolescents lack a stable home and good role models, they tend to look for these qualities outside the home. For many youth, gangs provide role models and fulfill the needs of a loving family. Erica, who joined a gang when she was fifteen, told researcher Jody Miller that "In some ways [being in the gang] makes me feel like a person, like actually somebody." Gangs promise to give their members love, respect, companionship, understanding, and security, and for Erica, relationships that she did not have outside the gang. "People trust me and I trust them. It's like that bond that we have that some of us don't have outside of that. Or didn't have at all. That we have inside of that gang, or that set."

Gangs may provide their members with a sense of belonging and a safe refuge, but they also force gang members to give up their individual identities and the freedom to act however they choose. Julie, a teen who hung out with gang members but refused to join herself, explained to Miller why she refused to join a gang:

Just, like, I can hang out, I mean, if I was a Crip I couldn't hang out with some of my friends that are Bloods 'cause they don't get along. And just, I guess, being able to hang out with who I want. And, wearing what color I want. I

mean, that's stupid that, in a certain gang you're not allowed wearin' a certain color.

While many gang members join gangs to find a surrogate family, the
gangsters tell researchers that the most important reason they joined the
gang was for protection. Gang neighborhoods are frequently dangerous
places for both gang and nongang members. Gangs today are more dangerous than gangs of the 1950s and 1960s. Fights that once involved on-
foot forays into enemy territory using fists, brass knuckles, and knives
have become increasingly lethal due to the easy availability of guns and
cars used in drive-by shootings.

Teens who are not gang members are continually harassed and
beaten by those who are. Tired of being constantly questioned about their
gang loyalties—and taken for a gang member by rival gangs—some adolescents decide they might as well join the gang. James D. Vigil quotes a
young teen who explains why he decided to join a gang: "It was either get
your ass kicked every day or join a gang and get your ass kicked occasionally by rival gangs."

Gangs do provide some protection for their individual members.
Heather, a girl gangster quoted by Miller in *One of the Guys: Girls, Gangs,
and Gender*, explains that "not as many people mess with you" as a gang
member. Gang members know that they are not alone in any confrontation, that the gang is there to watch their backs. And if a gangster is at-
tacked or "disrespected," he or she is assured that members of his or her
gang will retaliate against the offending gang.

But while gang members feel the gang protects them from violence,
in actuality, gang membership actually increases the potential for a violent confrontation. The violence starts with a member's initiation into
the gang. Initiates are frequently "beaten in" or "jumped in." Jerry, an
eighteen-year-old Thundercat gang member, tells Decker and Van Winkle
how his gang initiates someone:

> He's gotta wear all blue and stand in a circle and everybody
> just rush him all at one time and then back off of him and
> see if he still standing. If he drop he got to get back up and
> take it again. That's how you initiate a man.

Some initiates are required to fight or kill a rival gang member. And taking revenge against an attack on or disrespect against a fellow member
just leads to a never-ending cycle of violent retaliation. Some teens tell researchers that violence is a deterrent for joining a gang. As some teens
told Miller, joining a gang "won't do anything but get you killed."

Gang experts agree that there is rarely one single reason to explain
why a teen decides to join a gang. Joining a gang is usually the result of
a complex set of factors that all contribute in one way or another to a person's decision. A desire for family and protection are just two of the many
reasons that may influence youth to join gangs. *At Issue: What Encourages
Gang Behavior?* examines some of the conditions that contribute to an
adolescent's decision to join a gang, as well as some factors that influence
gang behavior.

1

Youths Join Gangs for Many Reasons

Lonnie Jackson

Lonnie Jackson, the director of Minority Services for the Oregon Youth Authority, developed a gang prevention program while working at the MacLaren Youth Correctional Facility. He is the author of Gangbusters: Strategies for Prevention and Intervention.

There are many reasons why some teenagers believe that gangs are a reasonable and even attractive improvement in their lives. Problems with their families or social environment are the main factors that influence teens to join gangs. Teens who become involved in gangs frequently do not have positive role models at home and often have an unstable family life. They also tend to live in communities where crime and violence are the norm and where there is little economic opportunity. Gangs look attractive when teens see that selling drugs gives them the opportunity to support themselves and satisfy their urge of instant gratification for material wants. In addition, gangs often hold tremendous power in their neighborhoods, and teens may join a gang for protection or because they are attracted to the power.

Although some young people dress their infants in gang colors and take pictures of them with their little fingers curled and bent as if flashing gang signs, the vast majority of today's gang members were not born into their gangs. Their association with gangs was a choice they made—a choice made attractive for a number of reasons.

Why gang involvement seems reasonable

To put together an effective intervention or counseling strategy for these youths, we first must examine factors that make gang involvement seem a reasonable, if not attractive, way to improve their lives. In dealing with gang-affiliated youth, we have found similarities in the backgrounds of those who join gangs.

A young person may become involved in a gang for these reasons:

1. Frequent exposure to crime and violence during formative years results in desensitivity to such occurrences.
2. There are few positive role models, particularly of their own ethnicity; negative influences are more common than positive ones.
3. They come from unstable families, with very little parental control.
4. They live in an environment lacking economic activity conducive to lawful self-sufficiency; instead, the environment breeds hopelessness and offers few reasons to believe success can be achieved through conventional means.
5. Their environment lacks constructive social and recreational activities for them.
6. Their social environment has a distorted set of moral values in which selfish, antisocial conduct is accepted and promoted as the acceptable norm.
7. The youth believe that they have matured as far as possible; that there is not much more to look forward to except what they perceive as "low-level" jobs.
8. They are entrapped into selling drugs by the lure of "living large," despite inadequate skills, education, or qualifications.
9. They inhabit a culture that highly values immediate gratification, both materially and sensually.
10. They suffer from low self-esteem.
11. There is an absence of respected adult figures to give youths the "right word," or to affirm traditional values and standards, and to encourage the youths to keep their conduct within bounds.
12. There is a natural need to ensure physical safety, to have a sense of belonging, and to form secure emotional relationships with others.
13. Because they feel insignificant and powerless, youths are attracted to the power of gangs because gangs exercise considerable control over the lives of others and command the attention of public officials and the news media.

A few words of caution are in order before we proceed. First, the vast majority of young African Americans and an increasing number of children of all races and socioeconomic conditions are exposed to one or more of these factors and never join gangs. So, while there is some cause and effect between these factors and gang involvement, this author is not suggesting that African-American children and their families cannot resist or overcome them.

Second, none of these factors is a justification for antisocial behavior. In fact, to encourage anyone to regard them in that light would perpetuate the problems we seek to eliminate. Having said that, let us consider how each of these factors, over time, might cause youths to regard more conventional, wholesome lifestyle choices to be unrealistic, even undesirable, for them.

Factors leading to gang involvement

Factor one: Frequent exposure to crime and violence during formative years, results in desensitivity to such occurrences.

Reasonable people disagree about whether violence on television and in movies causes people to commit violent acts. However, few dispute the fact that the more one is exposed to traumatic and violent events, the less unusual and less disturbing they become.

After years of having sleep interrupted by sirens and gunfire and seeing dead bodies surrounded by onlookers on the streets of his neighborhood, a child may come to regard violence as natural and unavoidable. He may come to feel violence is no big deal, especially if the adults in his home are violent towards him and each other. If he has been beaten up at home and at school, and no place is safe, why not take one more "beatdown," a common gang-initiation, in order to be somebody?

Once in the gang, he may see no reason not to hurt others. "I might as well get mine while I can. What difference does it make if I have to take somebody out to get paid? Nobody lives forever. Besides, my homies got my back."

Factor two: There are few positive role models, particularly of their own ethnicity; negative influences are more common than positive ones.

When children's parents, relatives, or close family friends are enjoyably engaged in an activity, the children are more likely to want to attempt it themselves. They gain confidence that they, too, can accomplish it. These successful adults are role models for the children.

> *Many of today's gangsters . . . grew up without their fathers or any other permanent adult male in their home or in their lives.*

Many professionals are in the same profession as one of their parents, such as Liza Minnelli, Natalie Cole, Ken Griffey, Jr., and Barry Bonds, as well as many teachers and police officers. Many of today's gangsters do not have such role models. Most grew up without their fathers or any other permanent adult male in their home or in their lives.

Charles Barkley was right when he said in a television commercial, "I am not a role model. I am not paid to be a role model. Just because I can play basketball doesn't mean that I should raise your kids." Lost in the hoopla over the commercial was the distinction Barkley and Nike were making between sports heroes or heroes in other endeavors, and role models.

A role model is someone who a person can relate to in intimate person-to-person moments, not under the glare and spotlight of publicity. The modeling must be authentic to be effective. Well-known self-improvement lecturer and author Anthony Robbins encourages the frequent practice of "modeling" to anyone who wants to maximize their potential and experience success in personal and professional endeavors.

Before anyone can be successful, or even begin to pursue a goal, he or she must believe that the goal can be attained. Young people are most likely to chose a model who looks like them, sounds like them, and appears to be facing the same obstacles and injustices as they are encountering.

We understand that many, if not most, of the youths we encounter do not know many people who have attained success through conventional or lawful means. More often, they see financial and professional success as something conservative white people control and deny to African-American people and others, like themselves.

With no one to serve as proof of their own potential, they readily respond to people who look and sound like them and appear to face the same obstacles and injustices in life. Many of these people reinforce the negative messages the youths have heard throughout their formative years about societal and other barriers to having a good life. Believing that the menu of their life's options is very short, they choose a direction that they believe will improve their condition.

Family

Factor three: They come from unstable families, with little parental control.

Most of the youth we see do not regard their parent, who most often is a single mother, as a role model. In fact, the parent(s) generally have no ability to influence the actions or decisions of their children. After repeated failure, many parents stop trying to help their children lead productive lives.

We do not want to place unfair blame on parents. Often, these youths are raised in single-family homes with the mother as the sole provider. She often faces serious economic problems. She may not be well educated herself, and it is likely that her salary does not meet her family's financial needs. She may hold more than one job. She may not have the time she needs or wishes she had to take care of her kids. She may go to work before her children are up and not return home until after the school day has ended. She may be on welfare, and her checks may be inadequate to meet her family's needs. When she tries to find a job, she may discover that she makes less, not more, after taxes are taken out of her paycheck than she has made on welfare.

> *The parents generally have no ability to influence the actions or decisions of their children.*

She also may have other personal issues. She probably does not have the financial resources to get her children tutoring if they need extra help in school. She might not be able to afford the fees to get her children into sports and, even if she can, she may not have transportation to get them to and from practices and games. Because they are exposed to television, her children may want things she cannot afford; so, they may become angry or find illegal ways to get what they want. Besides, the parent may have been a teenager when her children were born and never may have had positive role models to show her what good parenting involves. Then, after working hard all week, the mother may feel that she deserves weekends off and may visit friends, and leave the children unsupervised.

By the time our youths were big enough and bold enough to lie, conceal, and even physically strike back at their parents, these youths have exercised more overt control over their parents' households than their parents have. After losing one power struggle after another to their children and realizing the children do not want help or guidance, the parents simply may concede defeat to hold on to what is left of their sanity. Perhaps more tragic is the family in which the parents are clueless because their child has honed the skills of distracting, manipulating, and lying. These are some of the conditions that exist in many young gang-affected youth's homes.

Environment

Factor four: They live in an environment lacking economic activity conducive to lawful self-sufficiency; instead, the environment breeds hopelessness and offers few reasons to believe that success can be achieved through conventional means.

While there are exceptions to any rule, the overwhelming majority of young gangsters come from economically depressed communities. Economic depression is nothing new to many African-American communities. Yet, as mentioned earlier, neither this, nor any other factor discussed in this chapter, should be considered a justification for gang involvement and criminal activities.

Once initiated, gangsters gain a sense of being somebody important in their world, someone able to handle serious responsibilities.

These factors, however, are influential in steering youth toward gangs. Building on previous discussions, one would hardly expect to find many positive role models where there is little day-to-day success. There are many good people in such communities, many of whom have been concerned about improving the lot of each generation long before the gang phenomenon arose. Yet, economic stagnation provides no fuel for optimism.

Factor five: Their environment lacks constructive social and recreational activities for youths.

For reasons already discussed, many of today's youths must look outside the family for role models and emotional support. Yet, in the environments we have described, there is a considerable lack of social and recreational activities for the youths. Again, this is not to say there are not some in every community, but clearly there are not enough to deal with the population. And many of the well-intended, youth-focused programs simply do not appeal to youths at risk for gang involvement.

Communities without a strong enough economic base to construct their own facilities for recreational and social activities must depend on municipal and county governments or an external benefactor to provide the facilities. This does little to create a feeling of community empowerment. However, it is better to have them, from whatever the source, than not to have them at all. There simply are not enough of them to meet the expanding population of youths in need of positive direction. With increasing pressure on all levels of government to stop growing and to cut taxes, we can expect less, not more, assistance from all levels of the government. However much they might want to help, financial restraints may prevent it.

Factor six: Their social environment has a distorted set of moral values in which selfish, antisocial conduct is accepted and promoted as the accepted norm.

Rational, pragmatic thinking is not valued among many youth today. Where their parents would consider it a negative statement about someone to say he or she is "screwed up," some gangsters use the Spanish word for crazy, *loco,* and proudly refer to themselves as "loced out," perhaps realizing that one must be a bit insane to voluntarily enter a world of "beatdowns," where they face the possibility of being a victim of a drive-by shooting.

For the sake of being part of something larger than themselves, they subscribe to a code of conduct which says that the worst thing you can be is "soft," or a "punk." They are indoctrinated to believe that the only people to care about are one's "home-boys," the members of their gang "set." They must not drop the exterior mantle of being hard, even when affirming their extraordinary allegiance to each other. They must look tough, intimidating, and angry, except when getting high on drugs or forty-ounce bottles of malt liquor in the security of the "set."

Being hard means you do not walk erect like some punk businessman in a "monkey suit." You keep your shoulders slouched and your head down a bit. You wear mostly black, very baggy clothes, so nobody can give an accurate physical description of you to the police.

[Thirteen-year-old gang members] are more likely to see a gun or vial of crack cocaine as means for immediate acquisition of the things they would otherwise never have—status and "bank".

So pervasive is this new cultural attitude of hardness among today's youth that from a very early age, many kids, even those with no desire to get into a gang, dress, walk, and talk as if they were gang members. This imitative conduct sometimes is motivated by a desire to be thought of as a gangster. Such kids are called "wanna-bes." In other instances, such behavior is motivated by a desire to be left alone. If they look tough, they reason, maybe the bullies will pick on somebody else.

Most gangsters have no regard for marriage, and in a warped sense of manhood, reinforce in each other the notion that it is a sign of weakness for a man to become emotionally committed to one sex partner. Girls and women are trophies to be seen with and tools for the release of sexual tension, often referred to in such terms as "bustin' a nut," "gettin' G'd," "knockin' the boots," or "gettin' waxed."

A youth who talks to such fellows about making a commitment, planning a family, or supporting his children and their mother is likely to lose standing with them. "Sex? Everybody's gonna do it. Just do not get involved emotionally—sprung on the girl—and go soft. Hell, if she gets pregnant, that's her problem."

Unfortunately, it is true that people from all walks of life would prefer to have sensual pleasure without responsibility. A child who sees his peers jumping off the springboard into the deep end of a pool all summer, experiencing nothing but pleasure, probably will decide that he at least wants to give it a try. And, in too many cases, there is no one to help him consider other options.

Employment

Factor seven: The youth believe they have matured as far as possible; that there is not much more to look forward to except what they perceive as "low-level" jobs.

Despite the fact that many gangsters could not find gainful employment, live independently, and be self-sufficient, they often have high absentee rates and act out at school. They eventually drop out, reasoning that school is for punks anyway. They do not need to be in school. They are men, ready to "live large." An expression commonly heard among today's youths is, "I'm getting paid," which means they are making money.

They sometimes will say that they want a job, and despite the fact that they lack the skills to qualify for most minimum-wage jobs, they will say, "I ain't goin' for no burger-flippin' job at Mickie D's."

This attitude is the product of a misapplication of self-respect. The reasoning is that, "I deserve to have what I want in life. I do not need any more education. I do not need training. I'm a man. I need money." This attitude would get a person laughed out of a job interview with any organization in today's society except one—a gang.

Factor eight: They are entrapped into selling drugs by the lure of "living large," despite inadequate skills, education, or qualifications.

Gangs welcome people who see no need to continue the pursuit of self-development. Once initiated, gangsters gain a sense of being somebody important in their world, someone able to handle serious responsibilities. The job description might read like this:

> Watch the backs of your homeboys against attacks from sucker crews in rival gangs. We got to do an occasional jackback or some other kind of dirt, but it's only to enforce our control of our turf, you know, the geographic area we be claimin'. Forget them sucka jobs! Sell a little crack from time to time to wacked out suckas and you be handling thousands every month!
>
> There is no clock to punch, but you gots to be ready at all times. Be there. Be down. You'll get to ride in Caddies, Benzo's, Beamers, Jeeps, you name it. They won't be yours, but that do not matter. You can have your hair in Geri Curls all the time if you want to. You be havin' all the hos you can handle. You be livin' large. Gold chains around your neck. Lots of money. You be clockin' them dolla's and kickin' it and loungin'! Here. Take this nine (millimeter gun). You can have it. You're down with us.

Cars, sex, money, protection, status. This is not a bad promise to a boy who has nothing.

Factor nine: They inhabit a culture that highly values immediate gratification, both materially and sensually.

By now, the details of every snowflake on this snowball rolling toward gang involvement should be quite clear. The foregoing factors all build on each other for a cumulative impact on the minds of many young men today. It seems useless to leave the ghetto to get away from them, however, because when it comes to this ninth factor, it does not matter where one is.

Turn on the television and watch any music channel, and you are likely to see music videos glamorizing pimping and making big dollars daring any sucker to "step to me."

Materialism and immediate gratification are themes repeated in most commercials on any broadcast, particularly for those the young men are most likely to watch, such as sporting events. Throughout our society, we constantly are encouraged to go for the gold, be young, have fun, and drink. Come on the show, spin the wheel of fortune, play the state lottery, and get rich now! Just do it.

These societal pressures appeal not just to youths, but also to their parents, who, with each passing day, are reminded of how little they have after so many years of living. Neither the child nor his parents is likely to watch religious or intellectually stimulating shows. The parent figure has no desire to feel guilty or inadequate, and would rather not sit through such a program. The child, in turn, has no reason or desire to sit and listen to it when something more sensually stimulating is just a click away.

Factor ten: They suffer from low self-esteem.

Few thirteen-year-olds are capable of earning a legal income to support their family. However, they are more likely to see a gun or a vial of crack cocaine as means for immediate acquisition of the things they would otherwise never have—status and "bank" (money).

Vandalism and intimidation are everywhere. In the face of this danger, even a "good" child might consider joining a gang to feel more secure.

Most human behavior is in direct response to how people feel about themselves. Those who feel good about themselves usually seek to do good for others. Those who have low self-esteem spend a great deal of time trying to cope with their feelings of inadequacy. Sometimes, they try to better their conditions. Other times, they try to get even with people they think unfairly acquired the things in life they themselves lack.

This is often the mind-set of the youth about to enter a gang. It seems that at every turn, society is telling him, as the Madam, Miss Brooks, said to Billie Holiday in *Lady Sings the Blues*, "You git on 'way from 'roun' here! 'Cause you ain't nothin'! You ain't never been nothin' and you ain't gonna be nothin!" Once internalized, such perceptions of one's own potential make fairly low lifestyles appear to be their only domain.

Factor eleven: There is an absence of respected adult figures to give youths the "right word," or to affirm traditional values and standards, and to encourage youths to keep their conduct within bounds.

Not that long ago, if an African American were found skipping school or misbehaving, an adult in the community would have grabbed him by the ear, gotten in his face, given him a brief lecture, a swat on the behind, and sent him on his way. The adult then would follow up with a call or a personal visit to his parents to give them the whole story. There was a kind of trust and a sense of shared responsibility in African-American communities. The Swahili saying, "It takes an entire village to raise a child," is a popular quote that once was visible in inner-city communities.

This has changed. Because of a number of factors, including the mobility of our society, wars, high rates of incarceration and homicide, and the irresponsibility and selfishness of so many adults over the past thirty years, many children do not have grandparents, uncles, ministers, or even coaches to steer them in the right direction or to simply let children know that they noticed their misbehavior and care enough about them to confront them and tell them to "get on the good foot."

Adults should be human barometers, responsibly regulating the behavior of the youngsters in our midst. Lacking responsible, caring adults, children are left to their own devices. Without role models, resources, or peers with self-esteem and good judgment, it is easy to see how the snowball picks up size and speeds toward gang involvement.

Self-preservation

Factor twelve: There is a natural need to ensure physical safety, to have a sense of belonging, and to form secure emotional relationships with others.

In many communities, sometimes hundreds of rounds of gunfire can be heard in the middle of the night. Vandalism and intimidation are everywhere. In the face of this danger, even a "good" child might consider joining a gang to feel more secure. This is not a uniquely American phenomenon, as children in South Africa, Northern Ireland, and Lebanon could attest. Self-preservation is one of the highest instincts in nature. However, the fallacy of this decision is clear: by joining a gang, one becomes a "mark," a target for harm from rival gangs.

The youths who join gangs often come from families who do not provide them with emotional stability and security. Often, they are from single parent homes with the parent absent a great deal of time. They often live in poverty and do not do well in school. Consequently, they feel lost and alone. They have few friends, no close family ties, and no adult looking out for them. In essence, they have no sense of belonging.

Gangs offer them what their family is not providing—a sense of belonging. In a gang, they have "friends" to turn to, people who will look out for them, people who will even die for them, if need be. They have someone to spend time with, to relax with, and often, for the first time in their lives, they feel they are part of something.

Factor thirteen: Because they feel insignificant and powerless, youths are attracted to the power of gangs because gangs exercise considerable control over the lives of others and command the attention of public officials and the news media.

If a youth wears an athletic Starter jacket, adults fear him, thinking he is a gangster. He gets beaten up by real gangsters or "wanna-bes" and his jacket is stolen. He calls the police. They take an hour to contact him, take the information, and leave, with no promise of a follow-up investigation. "Well," he reasons, "if you can't beat 'em, join 'em."

The youth feels that society does not care about him. Because many adults misunderstand, and even fear today's youths, many youths see themselves as part of the problem, even when they would rather not be.

To the extent they feel society has given up on them, they are willing to give up on themselves. When they do, another gang holds a reception.

As a gang member, he is now somebody. He can read about himself and his "homeboys" in the paper. When there's a "drive-by," the television cameras line up and interview people about their fear of gangs in the neighborhood. He feels he is part of something important.

Finally, he is getting some attention. He is somebody now. When he shows up in his "colors," people show respect. Unless he is shown where this kind of attention will lead—incarceration or death—he will continue to enjoy the power he feels he now has.

The need for early prevention

While this viewpoint was originally designed to help those working with youths who already have joined gangs, all of the factors discussed here need to be recognized and addressed when a child is first vulnerable to gangs. Community programs, educators, and other knowledgeable people need to recognize the attraction gangs have to children who fit the criteria outlined in this chapter.

If we address these issues with children who fit the profile of someone likely to be attracted to gangs *before* they join a gang, we will make giant steps toward eliminating gangs altogether. There is a tremendous need for prevention programs. To do this, we need the cooperation of corrections, educators, families, and the community. Children considered or identified as at-risk for gang involvement need mentors, tutors, afterschool programs, and counseling. Their families, including their parents, often need counseling and help from social workers. As a community, we need to provide hope and to show our young people that success and fulfillment can be within their grasp.

As stated by an article written by Donna Bownes and Sarah Ingersoll in the Office of Juvenile Justice and Delinquency Prevention's July 1997 *Juvenile Justice Bulletin:*

> As more communities attempt to prevent youth crime by developing and implementing long-term solutions, the demand for resources, best practices, and strategies continues to grow. If this country is to reduce delinquency and resultant criminality, there must be a coordinated, substantial, and sustained public and private investment of financial and human resources in families, communities, and the systems that support and protect them.

A parent and teacher education program is very helpful in prevention programs. Specific behavior can help identify a child as interested in gangs. Once identified, prevention efforts must begin immediately. Early signs include: displaying problems with family relationships; making little academic progress; having a high truancy rate; getting in trouble with school officials and police; drawing gang symbols on self and notebook paper; dressing in gang attire and making changes in hair style; playing "gang" in the neighborhood or on the schoolgrounds; using a new vocabulary; staying out all night; and living in a neighborhood that has gangs.

Programs listed in the Office of Juvenile Justice and Delinquency Prevention's July 1997 *Juvenile Justice Bulletin* that have proven effective include those that have included some or all of the following: counseling and intervention services, programs for parents that improve parenting skills, health services that provide prenatal care and health education classes, school-based programs that target at-risk behaviors, economic development and training programs including job readiness and skill development, law enforcement-sponsored programs, and comprehensive community mobilization activities.

2

Youths Join Gangs for Protection

Scott H. Decker and Barrik Van Winkle

Scott H. Decker is a professor and chair of the criminology and criminal justice department at the University of Missouri in St. Louis. Barrik Van Winkle is a systems analyst at the University of Texas at Austin. They are the authors of Life in the Gang: Family, Friends, and Violence.

The most common reason many teens give for becoming involved in gangs is the perceived protection the gang offers against rival gangs in their neighborhoods. Teens consider their fellow gang members as family who will look out for them and protect them from opposing gangs. Within the gang they believe that they are safe from attacks by other gang members, even though they are actually more likely to be involved in violent fights as a gang member. Violence plays an important role in gangs—initiations for many gang members consist of submitting to a beating by their fellow gangsters or committing a violent act against a rival gang member. Once teens have joined a gang, they still believe protection is the most important advantage of gang membership, although they also cite protecting the neighborhood and making money by selling drugs as reasons for staying in the gang.

There is considerable debate about what constitutes a gang and who qualifies as a gang member. Bursik and Grasmick (1993) identify two main approaches to defining gang membership; definitions that focus on gang processes (such as formation, recruitment, evolution, transmission) and those that focus on behavior (especially participation in illegal activities). Clearly, the criteria used to distinguish gang activity from nongang activity, gang members from nongang members, and gangs from other forms of adolescent organizations are of critical importance. In this viewpoint, we explore what gang members themselves consider to be the definition of a gang. Interestingly, there is as much diversity of opinion about this matter among gang members as there is among academics and criminal justice personnel.

We received no single answer to the question "What is a gang?" from our subjects. Reflecting the categories offered by Bursik and Grasmick (1993), subjects used both group process and participation in illegal behavior as the defining criteria for gangs. The most common element in definitions of a gang referred to its collective nature, an attribute offered by 92 percent of respondents. This underscores the salience of the group for defining a gang.

> Cause we all hang around each other and there is more than two or three of us and we stick up and hang in there for each other, do whatever for each other. It's a gang, it's a group of us anyway I think. We ain't doing nothing too positive. (Male #012, "Lance," twenty-year-old West Side Mob member)

> A group of individuals who set out to do not necessarily positive things. Just people who didn't do too good in life and are not doing too good now. (Male #042, "Leroy," seventeen-year-old Rolling 60's Crip)

> To my knowledge it's a group of fellas. Not just fellas but ones that can depend on each other that's all down for the same thing. Everybody think a gang ain't nothing but just thinking about being violent. Our gang, we think about working. Yeah, we sit in the parking lot and we drink. We try to get jobs and stay off the streets. We don't want to be known. We want to be known but we don't want to be known in no wrong way. We already got that impression now. We already known the wrong way. (Male #037, "Big Money," twenty-two-year-old Compton Gangster)

Violence

While most definitions of this nature began by focusing on the more benign aspects of association, the majority (69 percent) acknowledged the negative aspects of gangs, particularly violence. This was made evident by "Roach" (male #058, fifteen-year-old Blood), who first offered that a gang was "a group" and, when pressed, told us that it was "like family" but finally concluded that it was "Violence, it's violence." The role of threat was underscored in many of the definitions offered of gangs, often by noting the need for protection that the presence of rival gangs created. Indeed, 53 percent of our respondents specifically mentioned the role of threat in defining a gang. Sometimes threat was in the form of "disrespecting" a gang, actions that carried the implicit promise of violence.

> Well we call it a gang I guess because we all stick together and stuff and if somebody disrespect us we just come and retaliate. (Male #049, "Chris," seventeen-year-old Rolling 60's Crip)

> Bunch of us get together, really down for it. It's just like somebody go pick on him so we go after them, just like that.

(Male #053, "Jimmy," eighteen-year-old 107 Hoover Crip)

A large number of people period. Most of the time you with a lot of people you don't gotta worry about getting jumped. (Male #071, "B Daddy," seventeen-year-old Inglewood Family Gangster)

The need for protection took on added importance for those who had been involved in crime, creating enemies as a consequence of their criminal activities.

The most important reason for me is because I have a lot of people behind me. You never have to watch your back. If you have did a lot of dirt in your life, if you have done a lot of wrong things you have to watch your back cause no telling who want you. (Male #034, "Lil Gene Mack," eighteen-year-old 19th Street Rolling 60's Crip)

Family

These quotes highlight that the threat of being beaten up or shot by rival gangs was a consistent theme in most approaches to defining the gang. This was evident in the responses of individuals whose first characterization of the gang was as a "family." Twelve of the thirteen gang members who characterized their gang in this way indicated that the family character of their gang could be found in the willingness of members to look out for them or offer protection against violent threats from rival gangs.

It's more like a family away from home. You with your friends, you all stick together. They ain't going to let nothing happen to you, you ain't going to let nothing happen to them. (Male #031, "John Doe," sixteen-year-old Thundercat)

A gang is something you follow behind the leader. Do different things just like a family. Hang out together, rob, steal cars, fight other gangs like for competition. (Male #017, "Billy," twenty-one-year-old North Side Crip)

INT: What is a gang?
FEMALE #047, "Baby," fifteen-year-old Rolling 60's Crip: Like a family in a way. It's like brothers and sisters, like a family. There is more violence than a family.

Criminal activities

Finally, there were those who simply defined a gang in terms of its criminal activities. Seventy-four percent of our respondents indicated that this was a reason to define their group as a gang. While violence was primary among these activities, drug sales and other crimes often were mentioned as well.

INT: So the reason you call it a gang basically is why?

MALE # 101, "Money Love," twenty-year-old Insane Gangster Disciple: Because I beat up on folks and shoot them. The last person I shot, I was in jail for five years.

A bunch of thugs doing bad stuff. Some people good but they get in trouble and take it out on somebody else. Cause they devilish. They don't think before they do things, they just do things, they don't think. Regular people think. (Male #015, "Karry," fifteen-year-old Crenshaw Gangster Blood)

INT: What makes you all a gang?
WHITE MALE #091, "Paul," eighteen-year-old 107 Hoover Crip: The things we do. Fighting, shooting, selling drugs.

Many features of the debate about what constitutes a gang can be found in the responses of gang members to this question. However, it is clear that the individuals we interviewed focused on the more tangible issues in the debate, often defining their gang in terms of its role vis-à-vis other gangs. The group nature and cohesive aspects of gangs were consistent aspects of their responses. Regardless of how they initially characterized gangs, most subjects (74 percent) quickly focused on criminal activities—especially violence—as the defining feature of their gang. It is interesting to observe that, consistent with Klein (1971) and Short and Moland (1976), no subjects indicated a political orientation or agenda in defining their gang.

Pushed or pulled into membership

We now move to consider the reasons offered by gang members for their decision to join the gang. In every instance, joining the gang was the result of a process that evolved over a period of time, typically less than a year. In some cases, the process more closely resembled recruitment, whereby members of a gang would identify a particular individual and "convince" them to join the gang. This, however, accounted for very few of the individuals in our sample, fourteen out of ninety-nine. For the most part, the process of joining the gang was consistent with the formation of neighborhood friendship groups. Twenty of our respondents specifically mentioned that they had grown up in the same neighborhood as other gang members and had done things with them over a lengthy period of time. For these individuals, their gang evolved from these playgroups into a more formal association, in much the same way Thrasher (1927) described gangs in Chicago.

The process of joining the gang has two elements; the first is a series of "pulls" that attract individuals to the gang, the second are the "pushes" that compel individuals to join the gang. The pull or lure of gangs was an opportunity to make money selling drugs (a response offered by 84 percent of our subjects), to increase one's status in the neighborhood (indicated by 60 percent), or both. The primary factor that pushes individuals into gangs is their perceived need for protection. Again and again, our subjects described in considerable detail the threat they were under from rival gangs in nearby neighborhoods. A number of gang members (84 percent) found it impossible to live without some form of protection, typically finding such protection through their association with a gang. It is our argument that, for most members, both pushes and pulls play a role in the decision to join the gang. Four specific reasons were cited for joining the gang. In declining order of importance, they were: (1) protection, (2) the prompting of friends and/or relatives, (3) the desire to make money through drug sales, and (4) the status associated with being a gang member. The desire for protection is an example of a "push"—an external force compelling gang membership. The efforts of friends or relatives to encourage gang membership also represent a push toward gang membership. The other two reasons, desire for money and status, are clearly "pulls," or forces that attract individuals to gangs.

The family character of their gang could be found in the willingness of members to look out for them or offer protection against violent threats from rival gangs.

As noted above, most of the individuals we interviewed felt their physical safety was in jeopardy in their neighborhood; for the majority, moving to a safer neighborhood was simply not a viable option as few had the resources to effect such a move. Given these circumstances, most gang members (eighty-three) chose to align themselves with a gang for "protection."

> That is the advantage, protection. There wouldn't be all this stuff if certain people wouldn't try to be tough. So they try to be tough, so now we be Crips. They stay out of our business. Some cats from the city came over, that's how it all started. Jumped my friend. (Male #022, "8 Ball," fifteen-year-old 107 Hoover Gangster Crip)

> I thought about it [protection]; every time I walked somewhere people would try to start stuff. Yeah, like one time I got off my bus and these two dudes tried to double pin me. (Male #010, "Jason C.," fifteen-year-old Compton Gangster)

Few gang members acknowledged the fact that affiliating with a gang increased their risk of victimization. Indeed, some went so far as to state that being in a gang insulated them from fighting.

> It keeps people from fucking with me. So I don't have no trouble, no fights out on the street and all that. (Female #011, "Lisa," fifteen-year-old Compton Gangster)

Other reasons

And other gang members recognized the dilemma of not being in a gang yet having friends who lived in a neighborhood identified with a particular gang. "Bullet" decided to join his gang since he was seen as a gang member anyway.

Yeah, all your friends Bloods so you don't want to be the odd ball. Say I didn't become a Blood but I was always down with them and when dudes shot at us they was shooting at me too. Any way it goes, I was going to be a gang member. If dudes ride by shooting or whatever they will see me with them. (Male #060, twenty-year-old Inglewood Family Gangster Blood)

Similarly, "Smith & Wesson" reported that already being identified as a rival gang member also played a role in the decision to join.

I got tired of these Crabs saying what's up Fuz and I'm telling them I ain't in no gang. So I got in the gang. See what they do? (Male #057, fifteen-year-old Neighborhood Posse Blood)

Nearly a third (29 percent) of gang members reported that they joined because of the presence of a relative or friend in the gang. The process of recruiting friends and family members into the gang was seldom coercive; indeed most needed only minor forms of encouragement. Many gang members found their way into the gang through emulating a relative (#036) or friend (#054). One reported that he had joined, "Cause my brother was in it mostly" (#031). And another said, "Cause all my friends become one" (#010). Others indicated that it was a natural part of hanging out with friends in the neighborhood.

I ain't going to say it's going to be my life but it was just something that came up to me where I was staying. I was with the fellas and it just happened that I became one of them. I just got in the same stuff they was in. To me I see it as something to do. I can't put it a more better way than that. (Male #020, "Lil Thug," sixteen-year-old Gangster Disciple)

We have identified drug money and status as two of the factors cited most often as attractive features that "pulled" young men and women into gangs. As we document below, drug sales grew in importance once individuals joined their gang. However, only a small fraction (6 percent) were influenced by the opportunity to sell drugs in making the decision to join their gang. Others were more direct, stating that they found the money attractive or that money had initially attracted them to the gang.

My interest was in getting paid, man, strictly getting paid. I had a job at 13. I sold dope, cocaine, but it wasn't a career thing, it was like for extra money. (Male #040, "Knowledge," twenty-one-year-old Compton Gangster)

Girls are a frequent topic among adolescent males, and the opportunity to impress girls through increased status was cited by 40 percent of our subjects as the reason why they joined the gang. In this sense, their motivations closely resemble those of their adolescent peers who were not involved in gangs.

Yeah, you get respect, girls, money, drive around with your friends in fancy cars, saying stuff that nobody else know about. I wanted to be in cause they had the pretty girls and everything. (Male #015, "Karry," fifteen-year-old Crenshaw Gangster Blood)

But status concerns were not confined solely to the pursuit of women.

> It make me big, it make me carry guns, it made me like if somebody called and I tell them to come over and they don't come over I get mad cause I'm the big man, he supposed to come to me. I might pop them upside they head or I might pistol whoop them or I just sit back and just dog them out. Many things I can do to a person that they don't ask. (Male #018, "Maurice," twenty-year-old 107 Hoover Gangster Crip)

Process of entry

Typically, the process of joining the gang was gradual and evolved out of the normal features of street life in the neighborhood. Indeed, the imitative aspects of adolescent life are strong enough to suggest that most gang members affiliated themselves with friends from the neighborhood already involved in the gang. In describing how they came to join their gang, twenty-nine of the fifty-four who offered an answer to this question indicated they joined as a consequence of neighborhood friendships. On average, members of our sample heard about their gang while they were twelve, started hanging out with gang members at thirteen, and had joined before their fourteenth birthday. This suggests a gradual process of affiliation rather than one of active recruitment.

For the majority [of gang members interviewed], moving to a safer neighborhood was simply not a viable option.

Eleven percent of our respondents began the process of affiliating with their gang by being involved in fights. In these instances, they joined with friends in the neighborhood to fight rival groups in other neighborhoods before formally accepting membership. Violence is a hallmark activity for gangs and serves a variety of latent functions. It strengthens the bonds between existing members, increases the stake of prospective or fringe members in the gang, and serves as a means by which nongang youth come to join the gang.

> It was just when I was being around them they was cool with me and stuff so they just asked [me] to join in one time. They helped me in a lot of fights and stuff like that. (Male #093, "Lil-P," sixteen-year-old Crenshaw Mob Gangster Blood)

> I just went on a few posses,[1] I just started hanging around a

---

1. A "posse" is an incursion into the neighborhood of a rival gang.

> little bit with them but I was seeing the way things was go-
> ing and I wanted to join in so I initiated it by the hand signs.
> (Male #017, "Billy," twenty-one-year-old North Side Crip)

Another route to entering the gang stemmed from normal activities in the neighborhood. As such, becoming part of the gang is a gradual process, often the logical outgrowth of having gang-involved friends in a particular neighborhood.

> The people I hang with are all in it. You know like how you
> find yourself in a situation. (Female #047, "Baby," fifteen-
> year-old Rolling 60's Crip)

> I was hanging with them, it was just the area I was in was
> claimed by them so I just started claiming with them. (Male
> #025, "Tony," seventeen-year-old 107 Hoover Gangster Crip)

For others, school was the place where entry into the gang occurred. After all, it is not uncommon for friends at school to self-select into the same activities. Viewed in this light, the gang represents a "normal" feature of adolescent life.

Initiation

Becoming a gang member requires more than a decision. Most gangs require prospective members to undergo some sort of an initiation process. Over 90 percent of our sample indicated that they participated in such a ritual.

The initiation ritual fulfills a number of important functions. The first is to determine whether a prospective gang member is indeed tough enough to endure the rigors of violence they will undoubtedly face. After all, members of the gang may have to count on this individual for back up, and someone who turns tail at the first sign of violence is not an effective defender. But the initiation serves other purposes as well. In particular, the initiation increases solidarity among gang members by engaging them in a collective ritual. The initiation reminds active members of their earlier status as a nonmember and gives the new member something in common with individuals who have been with their gang for a longer period of time. Because of these common experiences, the initiation ritual—especially to the extent that it involves violence—creates aspects of what Klein (1971) has called "mythic violence," the legends and stories shared by gang members about their participation in violence. The telling of these stories increases cohesiveness among gang members. Further, mythic violence enables gang members to engage in acts they may otherwise regard as irrational, risky, or both.

Padilla (1992) reports the most common initiation ritual is being beaten in or "V-ed" in, a finding similar to those of Moore (1978), Hagedorn (1988), and Vigil (1988). Gangs in St. Louis also employ this method of initiation. This form of initiation included seventy of the ninety-two gang members who offered an answer to this question. While it took many forms, in its most common version a prospective gang member walked between a line of gang members or stood in the middle of a circle of gang members who beat the initiate with their fists. Falling down, crying out, failing to fight back, or running away sounded the death knell for membership.

> I had to stand in a circle and there was about ten of them. Out of these ten there was just me standing in the circle. I had to take six to the chest by all ten of them. Or I can try to go to the weakest one and get out. If you don't get out they are going to keep beating you. I said I will take the circle. (Male #020, "Lil Thug," sixteen-year-old Gangster Disciple)

Taking "six to the chest" was commonly reported as a means of initiation, especially by gangs who use the six-pointed star as one of their symbols, such as the Disciples.

> Well it's like this, if you around us and we recommend you to G, we just make up our minds and then somebody look at they watch we'll yell it's on, we'll initiate you. Then after you initiated you on the ground we pick you up hug you and say what's up G, just showing him that it's love. It wasn't that we wanted to rush you or hurt you nothing like that. It's meant because we want you to be around us, we want you to be a part of us too. (Male #036, "NA," eighteen-year-old Compton Gangster BIC)

The initiation fulfills other purposes, such as communicating information about the gang, its rules, and activities.

> INT: So that was your initiation?
> MALE #099, "Joe L.," eighteen-year-old Insane Gangster Disciple: Yeah. And then they sat down and blessed me and told me the 16 laws and all that. But now in the new process there is a 17th and 18th law.

A beating or a mission

Other gang members reported that they had the choice of either being beaten in or going on a "mission" or a "posse." A mission required a prospective gang member to engage in an act of violence, usually against a rival gang member on rival turf. Nearly a fifth of our respondents were required to confront a rival gang member face to face.

> You have to fly your colors through enemy territory. Some step to you, you have to take care of them by yourself, you don't get no help. (Male #041, "C.K.," twenty-two-year-old Blood)

> To be a Crip you have to put your blue rag on your head and wear all blue and go in a Blood neighborhood that is the hardest of all of them and walk through the Blood neighborhood and fight Bloods. If you come out without getting killed that's the way you get initiated. (Male #084, "Rolo," fifteen-year-old Rolling 60's Crip)

The requirements of going on a mission also may include shooting someone. Often the intended victim is known to the gang before the prospective member sets out on the mission.

> Something has got to be done to somebody. You have to do it. Part of you coming in is seeing if you for real and be right on. The last person came in, we took him over to a store. That person identified somebody out of our gang members that shot somebody. We told him that in order to be in the gang he had to shoot him. So he did. (Male #013, "Darryl," twenty-nine-year-old Blood)

> INT: How was he brought in?
> MALE #069, "X-Men," fourteen-year-old Inglewood Family Gangster: We asked him how he wanted to get in and he said he wanted to do a ride-by and shoot the person who killed his brother. So he did a ride-by shooting and killed him.

> INT: Was his brother a gang member?
> 069: A Neighborhood Piru Blood.

> INT: His brother was killed?
> 069: Yeah, that's why he wanted to be in. He wasn't gonna get in anyway but his brother got killed.

Gang members and their victims in such encounters are not always strangers, as seen in the case of a gang member who shot his brother, a member of a rival gang.

> INT: What did you have to do to be accepted as a member of the Rolling 60's?
> MALE #087, "Blue Jay," eighteen-year-old Rolling 60's Crip: Either kill somebody close to you or just shoot somebody, do harm to somebody close to you like family or something.

> INT: Which one did you take?
> 087: I shot my brother. He didn't know I did it.

Others told us that shooting someone, especially a rival gang member, as part of the initiation gave them "rank," higher status, and responsibility in the gang.

Alternative initiations

Six gang members reported an alternative means of initiation. Two members told us that they got "tagged" (tattooed) with India Ink and a needle or with a white hot coat hanger as part of the initiation process. Another gang member told us he was expected to sell a certain amount of crack cocaine in order to be accepted. Three gang members told us that as relatives of influential gang members, they were able to avoid the initiation ritual that characterized entry into their gang. These examples illustrate the adaptive nature of most of the gangs we studied; after all, for the most part, they were organized and run by adolescents. As such, we would not expect to find a rigid set of procedures to govern the initiation process.

In late 1991, we received a fax from city hall, advising the public of a new form of gang initiation taking place across the country. The fax described a process by which gang members drove a car at night with their lights out and followed anyone who flashed their lights at them. It was reputed that the gang members would then kill those individuals. We were skeptical about the validity of such claims, a skepticism shared by local law enforcement officials. At scores of local and national conferences, we have been unable to verify a single instance in which this process occurred. This incident illustrates the symbolic threat represented by gang members and how effectively the process of cultural transmission of gang images can work. The creation of images such as this leads to further isolation of gang members from social institutions and interactions.

The steps by which women were initiated into the gang varied considerably from those reported by men. While one, a leader of the G Queens, reported that fighting was the primary means of being initiated, other women said female members of her gang had the option of engaging in property crimes such as burglary or shoplifting. We did hear stories, exclusively from male gang members, that prospective female gang members were required to have sex with male gang members. Two male gang members illustrate that contention.

> Yes, they with it. For them [the Crippettes] to be down they got to have sex with us. One night one little gal and her friends were out saggin, she was a fine little gal, and she said she wanted to be down with us. She had to fuck everybody but I felt sorry for the little gal. (Male #033, "Larry," eighteen-year-old Thundercat)

> INT: Did she have to be beat in?
> MALE #084, "Rolo," fifteen-year-old Rolling 60's Crip: No, she got to poke everybody in the crew to get in. There was about 30 or 40 of us.

Female gang members, however, disputed this notion. Not one woman indicated she chose this means of initiation; indeed none could recall a woman who had. One woman's response, when asked about being required to have sex with members of the gang to be initiated, was laughter. This discrepancy illustrates the belief systems and bravado of adolescent males about their sexuality and control over females.

Reasons to be in a gang

We now consider what gang members regard as the positive features or advantages of gang membership. We presented subjects with twelve features of gang life, asking them to specify whether they represented a good reason to be in their gang. The responses to this question are found in Figure 1, where we list, in rank order, the percent of gang members who indicated that each category was a good reason to be in their gang.

Protection was identified as a positive feature of gang membership by 86 percent of the subjects, more than any other category. However, selling drugs and opportunities to make money were seen as advantages of gang membership by 84 percent and 82 percent of subjects respectively.

Defending the neighborhood also was viewed as an important reason to belong, as 81 percent of gang members responded in the affirmative when asked if this activity was a positive feature of gang membership. Interestingly, impressing people in the neighborhood, impressing friends, and impressing girls, all measures of status, received lower levels of support from gang members than did the categories just reviewed. In general, status concerns were endorsed as advantages to being in the gang by fewer members (thirty-eight) than were more instrumental aspects of gang life such as protection (eighty-three) or making money (seventy-nine). These responses reflect a preference for instrumental benefits of a more tangible nature than status concerns.

It is interesting to compare the responses to this series of questions to the answers gang members gave us about their reasons to join the gang. The desire for protection was the overwhelming motivation cited by gang members in their decision to join the gang. Their experiences in the gang had done little to change this. However, two notable differences can be observed between the reasons to join the gang and, once having joined,

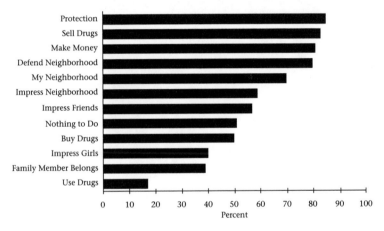

Figure 1. Reasons to Belong to the Gang

the advantages of membership. The second and third most frequent responses to the question "Why did you join your gang?" were the chance to sell drugs and make money. However, these categories received far stronger endorsements from currently active gang members as reasons to belong to their gang. At the same time, status concerns (ranked as the fourth most important reason to join) fell farther down the list as advantages to membership. This pattern suggests that once in the gang, instrumental concerns like protection and money assume even greater importance. In addition, it is no surprise that drug sales and defending the neighborhood received similar high levels of support. In a sense, these are mutually reinforcing categories, since successful drug sales require a secure turf or neighborhood base from which to operate. Thus, one way to enhance the profitability of drug sales is to protect the neighborhood, particularly against rival gangs that would seek to use a gang member's neighborhood as a location for selling drugs.

Many gang members who cited protection as a positive feature of gang membership echoed sentiments similar to those who cited this as a reason to join. There is a very utilitarian tone to these comments.

> It's like a comfortable feeling, you got someone to back you up and protect you. (Male #017, "Billy," twenty-one-year-old North Side Crip)

Those who noted the importance of the gang for making money have a similarly utilitarian perspective toward drug sales.

> There's money in a gang. I want to be in it, you see a lot of money in it man. That's why I really got in the gang, money and all. (Male #033, "Larry" eighteen-year-old Thundercat)

> You live in a neighborhood that's run by a gang you just can't up and start selling drugs getting they profit. They'll tell you. You either got to be in their gang or give them half of what you make or don't sell at all. (Male #038, "G.O.D.," nineteen-year-old Compton Gangster)

Gangs can "organize" drug sales in two important ways. First, some gang members have the economic capacity to "front" drugs that would allow an individual gang member to begin selling drugs or to make more profit than they could if they were independent of the gang. Second, and more importantly, gangs have both the will and the mechanism to use violence in order to control a particular turf and keep competing drug sales from interfering with their profits. The ability to accomplish these goals contributed to the large number of gang members who responded that making money or selling drugs was a good reason to be in the gang.

Despite these instrumental concerns (protection and making money), a number of members indicated that their gang fulfilled a variety of more typical adolescent needs—especially companionship and support. While we maintain that violence or its threat is central to understanding gangs, street gangs of the 1990s meet a number of the emotional needs of adolescents that do not differ much from those of nongang adolescents.

> One thing I like about gangs it's more people to be around, more partners to go places with. Like certain days we do, like Saturday and Sunday we go up to Skate King. Like next weekend we might go out to Northwest Plaza (a large shopping mall) and wear all blue colors. (Male #003, "Jerry," eighteen-year-old Thundercat)

> Social stuff and if somebody mess with you. You know you grow up into this shit. Mostly social. (Male #012, "Lance," twenty-year-old West Side Mob member)

Each of these quotes illustrates typical adolescent activities—hanging out at the mall, being in the company of friends, and engaging in "social stuff"—behaviors that resemble those of other adolescents.

References

Bursik, Robert J. and Harold G. Grasmick. 1993. *Neighborhoods and Crime: The Dimensions of Effective Community Control.* New York: Lexington.

Hagedorn, John. 1988. *People and Folks.* Chicago: Lake View Press.

Klein, Malcolm. 1971. *Street Gangs and Street Workers.* Englewood Cliffs, NJ: Prentice Hall.

Moore, Joan W. 1978. *Homeboys: Gangs, Drugs, and Prison in the Barrios of Los Angeles.* Philadelphia: Temple University Press.

Padilla, Felix M. 1992. *The Gang as an American Enterprise.* New Brunswick, NJ: Rutgers University Press.

Short, James F., Jr. and John Moland Jr. 1976. "Politics and Youth Gangs: A Follow-up Study." *Sociological Quarterly,* volume 17, number 2: 162–79.

Thrasher, Frederick. 1927. *The Gang.* Chicago: University of Chicago Press.

Vigil, James Diego. 1988. *Barrio Gangs.* Austin, TX: University of Texas Press.

3
Youths Join Gangs for the Thrill of Violence and Power

Isis Sapp-Grant and Rosemarie Robotham

Isis Sapp-Grant is a former member of the Deceptinettes, a girl gang in New York City. She is now a social worker who works with children who are at risk of joining gangs. Rosemarie Robotham is an editor for Essence.

A former gang member tells her story of how she became involved in a gang in New York City. She initially welcomed the friendship the gang offered because she believed no one else—including her mother—cared about her. While in the gang she committed many acts of violence and robberies against both the gang's enemies and total strangers. For awhile she felt a great sense of power because people feared her. However, with the help of supportive adults, she was able to leave the gang and turn her life around.

Her mother named her Isis, after the Egyptian goddess of fertility and protection, and, indeed, the young woman with waist-length dreads was once an adolescent to whom other teenagers paid a kind of homage and money for protection. She has become a woman since then—a statuesque beauty, her cheekbones finely etched, her dark eyes slanted upward, her skin a deep polished brown. Today Isis Sapp-Grant laughs easily, and yet there is a ghost of sadness on the high plane of her forehead, an unsurprised wariness in the depths of her eyes. A decade ago, she was the female leader of one of New York City's most notorious high-school gangs, the Deceptinettes, and violence was the routine of her day. Now 27, Isis has become a clinical social worker whose primary focus is young gang members. Though her history still pains her, she views it as the fire in which her life's purpose was forged. She shares her story in the hope that it will help others understand the forces that lure teenagers into the deadly spiral of gang violence.

I didn't set out to join, let alone start, one of the most fearsome girl gangs in the city. But there I was. Me and my girls, the Deceptinettes, sisters of the male Decepticons—Decepts for short. The name was inspired

Reprinted, with permission, from "Gang Girl: The Transformation of Isis Sapp-Grant," by Isis Sapp-Grant and Rosemarie Robotham, *Essence*, August 1998.

by a silly Saturday morning cartoon, *Transformers*, which pitted the Decepticons, who were the bad guys, against the Autobots, who were the law enforcers.

This was 1986, and I was 15 years old, living in Brooklyn with my mother, who was a social worker, and my three sisters, who at the time were 18, 14 and 2. My father wasn't around much; he and my mother were divorced. I'd just started at the High School of Graphic Communication Arts in Manhattan. My sisters were at different schools and, fortunately, they never got pulled into gangs. My personality was just different from theirs. I was more of a scrapper, always challenging my mother. As a kid, I thought I knew everything; I felt so powerful inside, and I couldn't understand why my mother didn't see that. She'd say, "Isis, why you always trying to act bigger than you are?" I craved recognition. So by high school, I was ripe for anything that would give me that feeling of power. And that turned out to be Decept.

Fighting for respect

The Decepticon gang started in the early 1980's at Brooklyn Tech, one of the top high schools in New York City. The male gang leader, Derek, aka Megatron, became my boyfriend at one point. He was an honor student before he eventually got shot in the head and became paralyzed. Like Derek, when I first got into Decept, I didn't have a clue I'd be in for that kind of violence. I was mostly thinking about protecting myself.

I realized quickly that there were a lot of violent kids at school. But if I acted crazy, they kept their distance. And I found that the crazier I acted, the more respect I got. Some of the other girls who were new to the school noticed it, too, and started hanging with me. We weren't really a gang. Just friends. But we let it be known that if you messed with us, we would fight back. And that's how it started. There were about ten of us in the beginning, but soon more girls joined us, and other kids in the school began giving us money to protect them. A lot of us lived in Brooklyn and knew some of the Decepticons. They would back us up in fights sometimes. After a while, we decided to officially join forces with the guys and call ourselves the Deceptinettes.

To get respect on the street, we had to act like badasses.

Our ranks grew to about 70 over the next three years—that's how long I stayed in the gang. In all, there were several hundred Decept members, mostly male, at high schools throughout the city. We called our main headquarters—Derek's school—Cybertron, like in the cartoon, and our favorite gathering place was this park we called Signs of the Times. We even had a hand signal that we copied from the cartoon. In the beginning, Decept meetings were just a group of mostly Black and Hispanic teenagers hanging with their friends. The only problem was, to get respect on the street, we had to act like badasses. And things just escalated from there.

The first time I ever robbed someone was on Halloween, a couple of months after I started high school. On this particular day, 50 or more Decepts decided to cut class and congregate in the park. And everybody was drinking Cisco and getting restless and mean. The next thing I remember, we went down into the nearby subway station and started racing up and down the platform and through the trains, robbing people, grabbing their stuff, beating them up if they resisted. I did it, too. I felt no boundaries, just this mad adrenaline rush. And at the time, I really liked the feeling that no one could mess with me. That I was invincible. Anything I wanted was mine.

I went home that evening with rings and gold chains and Louis Vuitton bags, and my mother didn't even notice. I knew she was having her own problems. I think she was depressed. Even though she had been a good mother to me and my sisters till then, she wasn't really paying attention to what I was getting into. And my sisters took their cue from her and left me alone.

Getting high on violence

That night I spread on my bed all the stuff I had stolen, and I was just amazed. I thought, That was too easy. After that, the violence really kicked in. And once it started, we couldn't stop because people were looking to get revenge on us, so we had to keep fighting just to protect ourselves. Plus, I think we really wanted to hurt people—as terrible as that sounds. We would play this game called one-punch knockout: We'd stand outside the subway station and choose somebody and try to knock them out with one punch. I was good at that. Or we would sit around outside the school—we hardly ever went inside for classes anymore—and come up with ways to just mess with folks. By then, our rep had gotten so far out there that most people just gave us whatever we wanted. It was at the point where we could close down any school by calling the school office and telling them Decepts were coming. People were that scared.

I really liked the feeling that no one could mess with me. That I was invincible. Anything I wanted was mine.

But they needed to be scared. We would get high on the violence. People were getting killed over the most stupid s—. I remember the first time I saw somebody die. We had beat up this boy's sister, and that night we were partying at some club. People were high out of their minds, and here comes this boy talking about "Leave my sister alone." This Jamaican guy I had a crush on—Frankie—he's like, "Just go away, man. You don't know what you're getting into. Just go." But the boy wouldn't leave, and some of the Decept girls started hitting him with baseball bats and hammers. Then the guys came outside and jumped into it, and one minute I saw the boy, the next minute I couldn't. They were just totally stomping him! Some guys fired shots, and all I remember was seeing the blood and thinking, this is all over hitting some stupid little girl.

I didn't know what to feel that night. I ran—we all ran—and found my way home in a blur. After a time, though, it didn't even matter. When you're in a gang, you see so much blood that you don't even care. It's almost like being a nurse. I would come home with blood on my shoes, blood on my coat, and my mother would say, "Where'd you get that coat?" And I'd say, "My friend gave it to me." Always some excuse. Then I'd go wash the blood off, wash my cuts and bruises—I never did get shot, thank God, and I'd think, Damn, she doesn't even see what's going on.

Forgotten youth

The way I felt was, no one cared about me and so I wasn't going to care about them. That's why I could watch somebody cry, plead, bleed, and it wouldn't touch me. It was as if we were all on a giant totem pole, and Black people were at the very bottom, and I was totally invisible. When you feel as invisible as I felt, you can become the most dangerous person in the world because you don't even care about your own life. I knew I wasn't going to live past 18. The only thing that gave me any pride was the fact that I was in Decept.

When you're in a gang, you see so much blood that you don't even care.

We actually had some very smart guys and some very intelligent and beautiful girls in Decept. One girl, Tangee, had been valedictorian of her junior-high-school class, and her parents bought her everything she wanted. But she was still missing something, and she was looking for it with us. Every one of us was troubled in some way. I was missing the mother I had known as a little girl. I had watched my mother struggling to raise us, and she was just beaten down from it, beaten down by life. She stayed inside her room most of the time. I didn't understand what was going on with her. She still went to her job every day, but when she came home she would withdraw, like she didn't really care what I was into. And I was so damn angry.

Another Decept girl, Nelsa, was the daughter of a heroin addict, and she had been taking care of her mother and younger siblings from the time she was 13 by working as a stripper. She would come from the club to school with a bagful of money, a fur coat and a gun. My best friend, Lisa, had been born in jail. She shuttled between foster care and her mother's house till she was 8. While living with her mother, she was abused—she actually looked forward to going back into foster care. Lisa could be just cold. If you messed with her in any way, she could hurt you without blinking.

Surprisingly, Lisa is now a high-school special-ed teacher, and a mother and wife. And Nelsa stopped stripping two years ago, started college and got a job in marketing. Lisa and Nelsa and me, we all got out. Tangee didn't. Tangee became a crackhead. I think of her now, wasted and strung out and abused, and I realize that could have been me. Except I never did crack. I wasn't into hard drugs like some of the other Decepts. I would smoke marijuana, and we all drank to get ourselves hyped up for whatever we had to do, but thank God I had the sense to stay away from cocaine.

The other thing was, I stayed a virgin. Lisa did, too. There were so many diseases out there, and we had been in so many abortion clinics with our Decept sisters, we wanted no part of sex. Don't get me wrong. I was a very horny little teenager, but I put it in its place. I realized that the girls who got "sexed into" the gang—the girls who slept with Decept guys to get in—they never got any respect. We had more respect for the girls who fought their way in. Because if you're in some street fight with a rival gang, you want some big, juicy fighting girls backing you. You don't care if they can have sex. You want to know they can fight.

All that fighting and stealing eventually got me arrested, of course. When I turned 16, I was picked up for robbing some girl on the subway. I remember being handcuffed and taken to jail by these two Black undercover cops who must have been the most gorgeous men I had ever seen in my life. And I was so embarrassed. The handcuffs were like chains around my wrists. I felt like a slave. In my head, I kept saying, This is not you. You are not really like this. But then this other thought kept coming: Don't fool yourself, Isis. This is you.

I was in jail for a week and a half. I called my mother from the precinct house. She said, "Little girl, these people you're running with, they are not your friends. You have no friends. Your only friends are your family." But I still didn't get it. I thought Decept was my family. I loved my Decept sisters and brothers. We would do things that families did, like go to the beach and have picnics, baby showers and dance parties.

But we also went to funerals together. Members of Decept were dying all the time. Others of us were drug addicts, still others were in jail with life sentences, and some girls had had two, three babies with no-account guys. I was getting tired of losing everybody one by one, and, beneath all the toughness, I was hurting.

Finding the will to live

By age 17, I was going to funerals every week. And then Frankie got shot. He was my heart. Walking home after his funeral, I told myself, This does not matter. But that night I went into my mother's room and climbed into her bed. I needed to reach out in the dark and know she was there.

The whole night I dreamed about Frankie. The next morning I thought I was still dreaming because my mother was standing over me, and I had the weird sensation that she was looking down at me in my casket. She was crying. She said, "Isis, I want you to live. I want you to choose to live. I don't want to bury you ten feet under. I want to see your children."

From that day, things began to change. I started showing up for more classes so I wouldn't get into trouble. But sometimes I'd just want to be with my friends, and stuff would start happening. If I said, "I'm going home," they'd be like, "Isis, you're selling us out."

When I did go to class, a couple of my teachers began taking an interest. One was my writing teacher, a Black man named Mr. Mason. He encouraged me to write about what I was going through in the gang. The other one was Mrs. Beasley, a tough little seventysomething Black woman. Most teachers at my high school were scared to death of me, but not Mrs. Beasley. She would challenge me to try harder.

One other person helped save my life: a cop! The first time John Galea saw me, the cops had pulled me in for a lineup; he cussed me out, called me a little hoodlum. But he saw something else in me too, because he kept telling me, "Isis, you're smart. You can do better."

So these three people hooked up with my mother and the principal of the school, and they came up with a plan. They told me that if I would go to class and keep out of trouble, they would allow me to graduate. They arranged for me to attend Fisk University, the well-known Black school in Nashville. We knew I had to get out of New York because all these people who knew I didn't have Decept protection anymore were calling my house every day, threatening my family. As long as I was there, my mother and sisters weren't safe. Well, I graduated. I went to Fisk and cooled my heels for a year. But I just didn't fit in. People in Nashville still saw me as this badass New York City gang girl. I wasn't that person anymore. My consciousness had changed.

So after a year I transferred to the State University of New York at Stony Brook, Long Island. I met my husband-to-be, Alphonzo Grant, there, a big football-playing, clean-living jock who is now a lawyer. He was so sweet to me, even after I told him my history. I think he fell in love with me because by then I had started to fall in love with myself. I was taking good care of myself, studying hard, majoring in social work. And I meditated and prayed a lot. I was beginning to understand that God had a plan for me. After college, I got married and later went on to earn a master's degree in social work at New York University. Life can be amazing.

Regrets

Still, I regret all the hurt I caused. People come up to me even now with scars on their faces or bodies, and they'll say, "Isis, do you remember me?" Some of them actually laugh when they say that, but most of them are really bitter. Like the woman I met in a store where I was buying shoes for my first job interview.

This woman holding a baby comes up to me and tears are running down her face, and she has this scar on her cheek and she says, "Isis, you don't know me, do you? You don't even remember what you did to me." And the horrible thing was, I didn't remember. I told her, "Whatever I did to you, I'm so, so sorry." She just stood there, crying and shifting the baby from hip to hip, and when she saw I still didn't remember, she said, "If I didn't have this baby with me, I'd kill you right now." And she walked out of the store.

There are faces I still see in my dreams, people we fought with who I later heard had died. I feel responsible because I was a part of the violence that killed them. But I can't change what I did. All I can do now is try to give back, try to make good on this promise I made to God. I promised that if I got out of my teens alive, if God spared me, I'd use my life to help save kids like me.

These days I do one-on-one therapy with kids at risk for involvement in gangs. I get referrals through the Madison Square Boys and Girls Club, and I work with the House of the Lord Church's community outreach program in Brooklyn. I do workshops in schools, and I travel the subways a lot and talk to the kids, because most New York City gangs still operate out of the subways. A whole new generation of Decepts is out there now, as well as other groups like the Latin Kings, the Crips and the Bloods.

I work mostly with gang girls; boys with these issues do better with male mentors. The truth is, every boy and girl out here needs a mentor to help them see what choices they can make, what programs they can participate in. If you're going to tempt these kids away from the thrill of violence—and violence can be an incredible high—you have to make them understand that somebody cares about them, that they are not invisible or powerless, that their life means something.

Parents in particular need to lay down clear guidelines, give their kids lots of reinforcement, and, most of all, pay attention to who their kids are becoming, who their kids' friends are, what interests them. None of us is perfect. We all get worn down by life sometimes. But we have no choice but to keep on trying to reach our children.

Looking back I see that my own mother never stopped caring, though she didn't always know how to help me. And the most important thing she ever did for me was to stand at my bedside that morning after Frankie's funeral, challenging me to live.

4

Girls Join Gangs to Escape Problems at Home

Jody Miller

Jody Miller is the author of One of the Guys: Girls, Gangs, and Gender.

It is much more likely that a girl will join a gang if she comes from a home with family problems, such as family violence, sexual abuse, drug and alcohol abuse, or a weak attachment to her parents. Involvement in a gang begins when the girl tries to avoid home due to the problems or dangers she encounters there. For many girls, the gang becomes their surrogate family and fulfills their needs for belonging and acceptance. Other girls join gangs because close members of their family—especially brothers—are gang members. In fact, many girls join a gang to be near their brother and to get his approval.

The family has long been considered crucial for understanding delinquency and gang behavior among girls.[1] Problems such as weak supervision, lack of attachment to parents, family violence, and drug and alcohol abuse by family members all have been suggested as contributing to the likelihood that girls will join gangs.[2] My study provides additional support for these conclusions, based on comparative findings from survey interviews and from young women's accounts of why they joined gangs.

Problems within the family

As Table 1 illustrates, gang members were significantly more likely to come from homes with numerous problems than were the young women who were not in gangs. Gang girls were significantly more likely to have witnessed physical violence between adults in their homes and to describe having been abused by adult family members. In addition, gang members were much more likely to report that there was regular drug use in their homes. Most importantly, gang members were significantly more likely to describe experiencing *multiple* family problems—with 60 percent describing three or more of the five problems listed in Table 1 and 44 percent reporting that four or more of these problems existed in their families. In fact, only *three* gang members—Angie, Brenda, and Chantell—said there were none of these problems in their families, compared to nine (20 percent) of the nongang girls.

Table 1: Problems Within the Family	Gang Members (N=48)	Nongang Members (N=46)
Witness to Physical Violence Between Adults	27 (56%)	12 (26%)*
Abused by Family Member	22 (46%)	12 (26%)*
Regular Alcohol Use in Home	27 (56%)	17 (37%)
Regular Drug Use in Home	28 (58%)	8 (17%)*
Family Member in Prison/Jail	35 (73%)	31 (67%)
Three or More Family Problems	29 (60%)	11 (24%)*
Four or More Family Problems	21 (44%)	6 (13%)*

*$p < .05$.

In addition, a number of gang girls had been sexually abused or raped in the context of their families.[3] In all, twenty-five (52 percent) of the gang members in my study reported having been sexually assaulted, and they described a total of thirty-five instances of sexual assault. Of these thirty-five incidents, twenty-three of them (66 percent) were committed by family members or by men whom the young women were exposed to through their families. Eight of these assaults were committed by immediate family members (e.g., girls' fathers, brothers, and in one case her mother). Eight were committed by extended family (e.g., girls' cousins, grandfathers, uncles), and seven were committed by individuals that young women came into contact with through their families. For instance, Tamika was raped by her stepfather's brother, Vikkie by her mother's boyfriend's friend, Yolanda by her uncle's friend, and Brittany by her aunt's boyfriend. While fewer nongang girls had been sexually assaulted (ten of forty-six or 22 percent), like the gang girls, two-thirds of these assaults (eight of twelve) occurred in the context of the family.

Gang members were significantly more likely to come from homes with numerous problems than were the young women who were not in gangs.

For many young women, home was not a particularly safe place. Turning to young women's descriptions of their decision to join a gang, it is not surprising that the majority (though by no means all) noted family problems as contributing factors. The ways in which family problems facilitated girls' gang involvement were varied, but they shared a common thread—young women began spending time away from home as a result of difficulties or dangers there, and consequently sought to get away and to meet their social and emotional needs elsewhere. Often young women specifically said that their relationships with primary caregivers were problematic in some way. A number of researchers have suggested that "the gang can serve as a surrogate extended family for adolescents who do not see their own families as meeting their needs for belonging, nurturance, and acceptance."[4] Regardless of whether gangs actually fulfill these roles in young women's lives, it is clear that many young women believe that the gang will do so when they become involved.[5]

Drug addiction and abuse

The most common family-related themes described by young women as contributing to their gang involvement were drug addiction and abuse.[6] While 58 percent of the gang members described regular drug use in their homes, ten girls (21 percent) explicitly discussed the impact of their mother's crack or heroin addiction. Drug-addicted parents, while not necessarily described as abusive, often were quite neglectful, leaving girls feeling abandoned and unloved, but also not providing necessary supervision over their time and activities. Moreover, given the intense degradation of many drug-addicted women on the streets, these particular young women likely dealt with the trauma of having knowledge of or even witnessing their mother's involvement in such situations.[7]

Keisha was fourteen when we spoke and had joined her gang the previous year. She described her neighborhood as "nothin' but Folks and Crips" and attributed her decision to become a gang member to her sense of abandonment resulting from her mother's drug addiction. She explained: "My family wasn't there for me. My mom smokin' crack and she act like she didn't wanna be part of my life, so I just chose the negative family, you know what I'm saying?" Likewise, Crystal described joining her gang at a time when she was "fighting with my mama 'cause she was on drugs."

Shandra got to know members of her gang "walking to school, back and forth to school and I would see them in the mornings and after school and after awhile I just [started] hanging around smoking weed and just kicking it with them." She elaborated:

> Right around the time that I started hanging with them I had just got put out of school and had tried to kill myself not too long before that 'cause I was just, you know, I had run away from home and I was just dealing with a lot of stuff. 'Cause my mother is on drugs real bad, and her and her boyfriend used to be fighting all the time and I just, I don't know, I guess I just didn't want to be around that. So I chose to be around the gang.

Shandra said after she "just used to kick it with them [gang members] so much, one day I just woke up and I just say I wanna be one of them, and then I told them and then they jumped me in the 'hood." She was twelve when she joined her gang. Shandra's mother knew she had become gang-involved "because I started coming in late and I be high when I came in, I started dressing like a gang member, wearing all stars and khakis and stuff like that." But she explained, her mother "didn't really say nothing about it." At the time, Shandra said she "felt close to" the other gang members and "bond[ed] with them like they [my] family." When she first joined, she continued, the gang was so "important for me that I did anything I could to get respect from the OGs and just, you know, be down for [the gang]. It was important because I wanted to feel, I guess, accepted to the gang, accepted in the gang."

Lack of supervision

In addition to their belief that joining a gang would fill emotional voids, a number of these young women said that a lack of supervision attributable to their mother's addiction also was a contributing factor. Veronica, for example, joined her gang when she was "gettin' ready to be twelve," after her older brothers had joined. She said the gang was "right there in my neighborhood . . . then I seen that my brothers, 'cause I seen my brothers get put in. So then I said I wanna be put in." At the time, she explained, "I was just doin' what I wanted to 'cause when I found out my mom was doin' drugs and stuff. So she wasn't never in the house, so she didn't know."

Likewise, Yvette explained, "My mama, she on drugs, [we] used to fight and stuff. Me and her don't get along . . . [and] my father, he just ain't been around." Yvette said because of her mother's drug habit, when she was growing up her mother often "made me stay out late and stuff like that." Eventually Yvette "just started hanging out with" gang members in her neighborhood, whom she described as also being unsupervised. "I just hung around with some people that can do what they want to do, stay out late, whatever, go home when they want to go home, I'm hanging out with them." She said, "It was like, I wasn't going to school a lot so I got with them. We was having so much fun. Most of them didn't go to school so I felt like I didn't need to go to school. . . . I had fun with the gang so I became one of them." Although her mother was unhappy and threatened Yvette when she found out about her gang involvement, Yvette said, "It was like too late for her to try and change me."

Physical and sexual abuse

Another theme that emerged in some girls' discussions of how they became gang-involved was the impact of being physically or sexually abused by family members. In most of these cases, violence and victimization in the family precipitated girls' decisions to avoid home, and several girls described running away from home and living for extended periods with friends—often exposing them to gangs. In a few cases, being placed outside the home as a consequence of abuse also had the unintended consequence of exposing girls to gangs and gang members. Erica's story is a case in point.

Erica was seventeen when we spoke and had joined her gang when she was fifteen. She lived with her father and stepmother for most of her childhood, until her father and uncle raped her at the age of eleven, whereupon she was removed from the home. Since that time she had been shuffled back and forth between foster homes, group homes, and residential facilities and had little contact with her family because they turned their backs on her. Erica explained, "I didn't have *no* family. Because of the incidents with my dad and my uncle. After that, they just deserted me and I didn't, I had nothin' else." Although she said her stepmother was the primary person who raised her, their relationship was severely damaged by the rape. "She doesn't, she doesn't believe it. I mean, even after he [dad] pleaded guilty she still doesn't believe it."

The most common family-related themes described by young women as contributing to their gang involvement were drug addiction and abuse.

Erica's childhood up to that point had been filled with violence. Her father was physically abusive toward her stepmother, herself, and her siblings, and as a young child, Erica had witnessed her mother being raped. Both her father and stepmother had spent time in jail, and there was heavy alcohol and drug use in the home as she was growing up. As a result, she described herself as a physically aggressive child. She explained, "In elementary school before I even knew anything about gangs, I'd just get in a lot of fights." In fact, her nickname in elementary school was "Iron Mike," in recognition of her Tyson-like characteristics. Her initial contact with gangs came when she was fourteen and living in a foster home. During her stay there, she met a group of kids and began spending time with them:

> I didn't know 'em, but I just started talkin' to 'em. And, they always wore them blue rags and black rags and all that. And, I asked them, I said, "Well you part of a gang?" And they tell me what they're a part of. So, it was like, everywhere I went, I was with them. I was never by myself. If they went out to [a] club I went with them. If they did anything, I was with them. And, um, we went down to some club one night and it was like a whole bunch of 'em got together and um, I asked to join.

Erica said she joined the gang "just to be in somethin'" and so that it could be "like a family to me since I don't really have one of my own." She felt that being in the gang allowed her to develop meaningful relationships. She explained, "People trust me and I trust them. It's like that bond that we have that some of us don't have outside of that. Or didn't have at all. That we have inside of that gang, or that set." Nonetheless, Erica expressed some ambivalence about being in a gang because it involved antisocial attitudes and behaviors that she didn't see as being part of who she really was, particularly as she neared adulthood. Her decision to join, however, was in part a search for belonging and attachment.

Likewise, Brittany described a terribly violent family life. She lived in a household with extended family—twelve people in all—including her mother, grandmother, stepfather, and an adolescent uncle who was physically abusive. Her aunt's boyfriend had sexually assaulted her at the age of five, but family members didn't believe her. Although she didn't know her father, who was in jail, she had early memories of him physically abusing her mother. Moreover, she felt very disconnected and unloved by her family and also described being isolated at school: "I didn't have no friends, used to always get teased. . . . My grades started going down, I started getting real depressed, started skipping school, smoking weed after school and stuff." Brittany saw the gang as a means of finding love. She explained: "I felt that my family didn't care for me . . . that when I was on the streets I felt that I got more love than when I was in the house so I felt that that's where my love was, on the streets, so that's where I stayed." And although she did not admit to doing so herself, Brittany noted, "My best friend got initiated [into the gang] by having sex with twelve boys."

Other factors

Other young women also focused on myriad family factors in explaining their gang involvement. Diane's experiences are exemplary of how family problems could compound in a way that ultimately leads to gang involvement. When we spoke Diane was fifteen and was among the most deeply entrenched gang members in the sample. She had joined her gang at eleven, but she was only ten when she began hanging out with members, including the seventeen-year-old young man who lived next door:

> I think I was about ten and a half years old and we started hanging out over there, over at his house and all his friends would come over and I just got into, just hangin' out, just becomin' friends with everybody that was there. And then I started smokin' weed and doin' all that stuff and then when I turned eleven it was like, well, 'cause they seen me get in fights and they seen how my attitude was and they said, "Well I think that you would be, you would be a true, a very true Lady Crip."

The time she spent with the gang and her decision to join were predictable results of her life history up to that point. As a young child, the family moved around a lot because her father was on the run from the law. Her father dealt drugs out of their home and had a steady stream of friends and clients moving in and out of the place. Exposed to crime and drugs at an early age, Diane tried marijuana for the first time at age nine. She noted, "I was just growin' up watchin' that stuff." Her life changed dramatically when she was ten and her father was sent to prison, leaving her care to her drug-addicted mother. Diane explained:

> We didn't have very much money at all. Like, my mom was on welfare. My dad had just gone to jail. My dad had just gone to prison for four years. . . . My mom was on drugs. My, see my dad, always sellin' acid, quaaludes, cocaine and my mom was on, just smokin' marijuana and doin' crack. Back then she was just real drugged out, had a lot of problems and it was just me and my little brother and my little sister and that's all that was goin' on, besides me goin' to school and comin' home to seein' my mom do whatever, hit the pipe, and goin' next door and hangin' out.

Diane remained very dedicated to her gang and fellow members, noting passionately, "I *love* my cousins [fellow Crips]. I *love* 'em." This was in large part because of what they provided her when she felt she had little else. She elaborated, "That neighborhood's not a good neighborhood anyway, so. I had nothin' to look forward to, but these people they helped me out, you know? I mean, I was a young kid on my own. . . . I was just a little girl, my dad's gone and my mom's on drugs." Diane's father had been released from prison when we spoke, but was locked up again—as was Diane—for an armed robbery they had committed together. Ironically, her close bond with her father, and the knowledge she'd gained from him about how to commit crime, had resulted in a great deal of status for her among her gang peers. She noted, "My dad is just so cool. Everybody, everybody in my little clique, even people that aren't in my set, just my regular friends, they all love my dad."

In addition to their belief that joining a gang would fill emotional voids, a number of these young women said that a lack of supervision attributable to their mother's addiction also was a contributing factor.

As these young women's stories illustrate, a multitude of problems within families can increase young women's risk for gang involvement. This occurs through girls' attempts to avoid home and to meet social and emotional needs, as a result of ineffective supervision over their activities and, in cases like Diane's, by showing young women through example that criminal lifestyles are appropriate. These problems are exacerbated when young women live in neighborhoods with gangs, which provide a readily available alternative to life at home. Moreover, older gang members appear "cool," and their seemingly carefree lifestyle and reputed familial-like bonds to one another are an appealing draw for young girls with so many troubles at home.

Gang involvement among family members

Some girls who lack close relationships with their primary caregivers can turn to siblings or extended family members to maintain a sense of belonging and attachment. However, if these family members are gang-involved, it is likely that girls will choose to join gangs themselves. Moreover, even when relationships with parents or other adults are strong, having adolescent gang members in the family often heightens the appeal of gangs.[8] As Table 2 illustrates, gang members were significantly more likely than nongang girls to report family members in gangs. Most importantly, gang members were much more likely to have siblings in gangs and were more likely to have two or more gang-involved family members.

These relationships were actually somewhat different in the two sites—with the relationship between girls' gang membership and that of her family being most marked in St. Louis. In Columbus, gang girls were not significantly more likely than nongang girls to have a family member in a gang—57 percent of gang members had family in gangs versus 48 percent of nongang girls. By comparison, all but one of the gang members in St. Louis (96 percent) reported having at least one gang-involved family member. In fact, a greater percentage of nongang girls in St. Louis (62 percent) described having a family member in a gang than did gang members in Columbus (57 percent). Moreover, St. Louis gang members were the only group for whom a majority reported having more than one gang-involved family member. In all, twenty-one St. Louis gang members (78 percent) described having multiple gang members in the family, compared to 38 percent of Columbus gang members, 29 percent of nongang girls in St. Louis, and 28 percent of nongang girls in Columbus.

Table 2: Gang Membership Among Family Members

	Gang Members (N=48)	Nongang Members (N=46)
Gang Member(s) in Family	38 (79%)	25 (54%)*
Sibling(s) in Gang	24 (50%)	8 (17%)*
Multiple Gang Members in Family	29 (60%)	13 (28%)*

*$p < .05$.

However, gang members in both cities were significantly more likely to report a gang-involved sibling than nongang girls. In all, 52 percent of St. Louis gang members and 48 percent of Columbus gang members had siblings in gangs, compared to 19 and 16 percent of the nongang girls in these cities, respectively. In St. Louis, nine gang girls reported brothers in gangs and ten reported sisters; in Columbus, eight gang girls had brothers in gangs and three had gang-involved sisters. Overall, 35 percent of the gang members had brothers who were gang members, and 27 percent had sisters in gangs. In addition, four gang members—two in each city—described having parents who had been in gangs.

Turning to young women's accounts of how they became gang-involved and the role family members played, there also are notable differences between the two sites. In Columbus, all of the young women who described the influence of a family member mentioned a sibling or siblings. In St. Louis, on the other hand, eight girls pointed to siblings, while twelve identified cousins or aunts who prompted their decision to join. Gang girls in St. Louis also were more likely to talk about the influence of *female* family members, be they sisters, aunts, or cousins. Perhaps as a consequence, gang girls in St. Louis were more likely to talk about the importance of their friendships with other girls in the gang, while most gang girls in Columbus identified more with young men.

In general, the greater influence of extended family members on girls' gang involvement in St. Louis was striking. The likely explanation lies in the socioeconomic differences between the two cities and their effects on the strength of extended family networks. As I noted earlier, the young women in Columbus tended to live in neighborhoods with higher than average rates of poverty and racial segregation than the city as a whole. However, the neighborhoods of girls in Columbus were somewhat better on social and economic indicators than the neighborhoods of girls in St. Louis. Moreover, while there are pockets of concentrated poverty in Columbus, St. Louis exhibits much larger geographic areas blighted by intense poverty, racial isolation, and population loss, resulting in large numbers of vacant lots and abandoned buildings in many of the poorest neighborhoods.

So how might these differences relate to the tendency for St. Louis gang members to say that extended family networks, rather than immediate family, drew them into gangs, while this simply was not the case in Columbus? I would suggest that the answer may lie in families' responses to entrenched poverty conditions. Research has shown that African American families living in poverty often rely to a great degree on extended family for economic, social, and emotional support.[9] Given the more detrimental economic conditions in St. Louis, it may be that extended family networks are stronger there than in Columbus. This would help explain why St. Louis gang members seemed to spend more time with their relatives outside the immediate family and, consequently, why those relatives had a stronger influence on girls' decision making with regard to gangs. Regardless of which family members have an impact, it is clear that having family members who are in gangs increases the likelihood that girls will perceive gangs as an appropriate option for themselves as well.

Siblings

More often than not, young women who joined gangs to be with or like their older siblings did so in the context of the types of family problems noted earlier. Veronica was a case in point. Her mother's drug addiction left her and her siblings unsupervised; when her older brothers began hanging out with the neighborhood gang, she followed suit. In fact, she went on to tell me, "Then my *little* brother wanted to get put in it. And he was like only about six. [Laughs] They told him no."

Violence and victimization in the family precipitated girls' decisions to avoid home.

Similarly, Lisa was thirteen when we spoke and had only recently joined her gang. Her brother Mike had been a member of a Folks gang for several years, and when the family relocated to another area of Columbus, he decided to start his own set of the gang in their new neighborhood. Lisa was among its members. Prior to Mike starting his own set, Lisa hadn't considered joining, but nonetheless said she "claimed [Folks] because that's what my brother was so I wanted to be like that too." Their mother had died when Lisa was eleven, and she described their father as physically abusive and distant. She felt very close to her brother and said her desire to be with him was her primary reason for joining his gang.

Several weeks before Lisa joined, her brother's girlfriend Trish—who was also Lisa's best friend—was initiated. Lisa explained, "One day Trish was like, 'Well you wanna be true?' And I was like, 'Yeah.' And they was like, 'All right.' And they took me behind the railroad tracks and kicked the shit outta me and I was in it [Laughs]." Lisa was initiated into the gang on the same day as her boyfriend and another male friend of theirs. A primary concern for her was to make a good impression on her brother. She explained:

> The boys was scared. They was like, "Man, I don't know, I don't know." And then I was like, I just looked at my brother. Then I looked at my friend and I looked at them boys and I was like, "I'll go first." So I just did it, I think . . . why I did it then is just to be, I don't know. Just to show them, my brother, that I was stronger than them boys.

Although she enjoyed what she described as the "fun and games" that she had with her brother and the other gang members, Lisa was actually ambivalent about being in a gang. She told me, "Right now I wish, I kinda wish I never got into it but I'm already in it so, like, um, I just, I don't know. I don't think I'm gonna be that heavy as my brother is, like all the time, you know, yeah, yeah." Lisa was especially concerned for her brother, who took his gang involvement quite seriously, which she perceived as putting his physical safety at risk. She explained, "My brother, when he was little, he was a little geeky little kid that wore glasses. But now he's like, you know, and I don't understand it but uh, I wish he was still a little kid that wore glasses." Nonetheless, she felt being in the gang allowed her to spend time with him. She surmised, "We all just hang out all the time. We just are always together. If you see me you see my brother. If you see my brother you see his girlfriend. If you see me you see my boyfriend. I mean, it's just like that."

It is clear that having family members who are in gangs increases the likelihood that girls will perceive gangs as an appropriate option for themselves as well.

In fact, a number of young women described joining their gangs in order to be around and meet the approval of their older brothers regardless of whether—like Lisa and Veronica—they had family problems at home. When Tonya was younger, she said she noticed "my brother just started wearing red all the time, all the time." She continued, "then after school . . . he just kept going outside. All these dudes and girls used to have fun, selling drugs and having money and stuff. And then I just wanted to do it. I thought it would be fun so I joined. I tried to join and then my brother let me join." Tonya said her initiation into the gang involved "just a couple of my brother's friends, he didn't let nobody really [cause me] pain for real, like really beat me up. They was just beating me up so I would have to fight back. I had some bruises, busted lip, in another minute it was gone, it was cool." What wasn't gone was Tonya's belief that "I had gained my brother's respect and stuff." Only thirteen at the time, she said "in the beginning I was like a little shortie. I didn't sell drugs, I didn't run around shooting or none of that." Her involvement increased, however, when she began "going out with one of my brother's friends," who provided her with drugs, which, she said, was "how I started selling dope."

Monica was also thirteen when she joined her brothers' gang. She had four older brothers, between the ages of twenty and twenty-eight at the time she joined, all of whom were members of the same Crips set. Sixteen at the time we spoke, she remained the youngest member of her gang and said she joined because she "wanted to be like" her older brothers. Monica described that she "always followed them around" and explained, "All four of my brothers were in so I was like, 'all right, I wanna be in a gang.' So I used to ride around with them all the time. And then my brother asked me, he said, 'Do you wanna be down or what?'. . . And I was like, 'Fine, I'll do it.' So I did." Perhaps because of the adult role models in her family and because she "grew up around it," Monica, like Diane, was one of the most committed—and consequently delinquent—gang members that I spoke with. She told me, "I'm down for real, I'm down for life." Diane's strong gang commitment resulted from gang members filling a caregiving niche unavailable to her from her family while her father was in jail. In contrast, Monica's commitment was the result of her close bonds to her family.

Extended family members

A number of the young women in St. Louis, as I noted earlier, described the influence of extended family members—most often cousins, but sometimes also aunts. All of these young women talked about spending quite a bit of their time at their relatives' homes, sometimes but not always when they lived in the same neighborhoods. Trina joined her gang when she was eleven; both her cousins and aunts were members, and she described "just being around over there, being around all of them" growing up. Trina said her aunts and cousins had dressed her in gang colors from the time she was young, and she surmised, "I just grew up into it."

Likewise, Shiree described her gang as "a family thing," and Alecia also said her gang involvement was "like a family thing." Alecia explained, "My auntie first moved on [the street] where I live now . . . [and] I started visiting my cousin." The gang evolved from "everyone that was growing up in that 'hood. . . . I seen all my relatives, not my father and mother, but you know, all my relatives in it and then I came over just like that." She said, "It ain't like they talked me into it or nothing." But eventually she and her mother and siblings moved to the same block, further solidifying her gang affiliation.

Vashelle said she joined her gang "because my family, all of my cousins, my relatives, they was Bloods already and then I moved over there because my cousin was staying over there so I just started claiming [the gang]." While in general Vashelle believed that girls joined gangs for "little stuff, they want a family or something," she argued that these were not her own motives. She explained, "It's just something I wanted to do because my cousin was in it so I wanted to be hanging around. . . . I ain't no follower. It's something I wanted to do and by them doing it was just more influence on me."

In some cases conflict in girls' immediate families increased the time they spent with relatives. Vickie began spending time with a gang-involved cousin when she became frustrated at home and "just wanted to get out of the house." She explained, "My mama always wanted me to babysit. I got tired of doing that. She always yell and stuff, she come home from work and start yelling. Like that kind of stuff and I got tired of hearing that. I need somebody to hang out with where I wouldn't be home half of the time." She turned to her cousin and "just started hanging out with him." The members of his gang, she said, "was like, 'you gonna do something [to join]?' I was like, I just gotta do what I gotta do," and so she joined.

> *A number of young women described joining their gangs in order to be around and meet the approval of their older brothers regardless of whether . . . they had family problems at home.*

As the preceding stories have illustrated, in some cases girls' trajectories into gangs are more heavily influenced by neighborhood dynamics, in others by severe family problems, and in still others by close ties to gang-involved family members. Dionne is perhaps the best illustration of how all of the factors I've described thus far—neighborhood context, family problems, and gang-involved family members—can come together to fuel girls' gang involvement. Dionne grew up in a housing project with gangs, where she had four male cousins who were members. She had been physically and sexually abused repeatedly by her mother's boyfriend, who was also her father's brother.[10] She explained:

> When [I] was little my uncle tried to have sex with me and stuff. I was like eight or seven, you know, and I told my mama in her sleep. I told my mama what happened, I woke her up out of sleep. You know she told me, she say, I'll get him when I wake up. For real, when she woke up, he ain't do nuttin' but tell her, "Aw, she lyin'. She just wants some attention." You know, and she hit me 'cause, you know, she thinkin' I'm just sayin' somethin'. I was mad though, and he thought he could take advantage by keep on doin' it.

There was also drug and alcohol abuse in the home, her mother had spent time in jail, and her mother and mother's boyfriend were violent toward one another. Dionne noted, "My mama, you know, me and my mama didn't get along. . . . My uncle [her mother's boyfriend], you know, we didn't get along. It was like, you know, he couldn't stand me, I don't know why. . . . He told me to my face, 'I hate you,' he say, 'I hope you die.'" Consequently, Dionne said "I used to like goin' to school, 'cause to get away from home." Eventually she began running away and spending time on the streets around her housing project with her cousins and other gang members. "I just started hangin' with 'em and doin' what they did then, and they, it was like, they, you know, was used to me hangin' around." When she was eleven, one of her cousins tattooed the gang's name and her nickname on her forearm. Dionne was drunk when her cousin tattooed her, but she said that afterwards the tattoo "made me feel big and stuff, you know?" While she was abused and felt neglected and disparaged at home, Dionne said being with the gang "be kinda fun, you know, bein' around all your little friends, just chillin' or somethin'."

Notes

1. See Canter, "Family Correlates of Male and Female Delinquency"; Cernkovich and Giordano, "Family Relationships and Delinquency"; Hagan et al., "The Class Structure of Gender and Delinquency"; Hagan et al., "Class in the Household"; Joe and Chesney-Lind, "'Just Every Mother's Angel'"; Moore, *Going Down to the Barrio;* Singer and Levine, "Power-Control Theory, Gender, and Delinquency"; Smith and Paternoster, "The Gender Gap in Theories of Deviance."

2. Joan Moore documented myriad factors within families that contribute to the likelihood of gang involvement for young women. These include the following: childhood abuse and neglect, wife abuse, having alcohol or drug addicts in the family, witnessing the arrest of family members, having a family member who is chronically ill, and experiencing a death in the family during childhood. Her conclusion, based on comparisons of male and female gang members, is that young women in particular are likely to come from families that are troubled. See Moore, *Going Down to the Barrio.* Mark Fleisher's ethnographic study of gangs in Kansas City, Missouri, documents intergenerational patterns of abuse and neglect, based on his observations of the interactions of gang members, their young children, and their parents. See Fleisher, *Dead End Kids.*

   Joe and Chesney-Lind observed that the young women they spoke with sometimes had parents who worked long hours or parents who were unemployed or underemployed—circumstances that they suggest affected girls' supervision and the quality of their family relationships. See their "'Just Every Mother's Angel.'" Esbensen and Deschenes, in a multi-site study of risk factors for delinquency and gang behavior, found that lack of parental supervision was associated with gang membership for male and female gang members but that maternal attachment was more predictive of gang membership for males than females. See Esbensen and Deschenes, "A Multi-Site Examination of Gang Membership."

   Bjerregaard and Smith found that neither parental supervision nor parental attachment was significantly correlated with gang membership for girls. However, it may be that these factors, particularly parental attachment, are not accurate measures of family problems. For instance, a number of young women in my study described feeling close to adults in their family despite abuse and mistreatment. Perhaps the most profound example was Sonita, who spent much of her childhood in various foster homes because of her mother's drug addiction and time in jail. Moreover, Sonita spent over a year on the streets as a runaway, which is when she joined her gang, and had been sexually assaulted by both her father and brother. When asked questions about her family, however, Sonita described her relationship with her mother as a close and trusting one and her family as one that had "a great deal" of fun together. This contradiction may partly be accounted for by the fact that she and her mother were in counseling together at the time that we spoke; nonetheless, it raises serious concerns about the extent to which attitudinal measures can adequately capture family dynamics.

3. These are included in my measure of abuse in Table 1 when a family member committed the assault, but not when it was someone else the girl was exposed to through her family.

4. Huff, "Gangs in the United States"; but see Decker and Van Winkle, *Life in the Gang.*

5. Perhaps this is why Esbensen and Deschenes found that although male and female gang members reported similar levels of commitment to negative peers, this was a stronger explanatory factor for gang involvement for females than males. See Esbensen and Deschenes, "A Multi-Site Examination of Gang Membership." There is some evidence that young women are more likely than young men to join gangs in a search for emotional attachments. For example, Chesney-Lind and Paramore ranked male and female gang members' perceptions of why youths join gangs, and girls' number one response was "family problems—to fit in and feel wanted and loved." In comparison, this response did not rank in the top five reasons young men listed. These included: (1) show off—to be cool and popular, (2) to have protection and back up, (3) to act bad, (4) to gain respect/think tough, and (5) peer pressure and influence. Nonetheless, the rest of female gang members' reasons paralleled young men's and included: (2) show off—be cool and popular, (3) to have protection and back up, (4) to act bad, and (5) to gain respect/think tough. It is important to keep in mind that these responses were not based on asking gang members to articulate *their* reasons for joining but to offer their perceptions of why "kids" join gangs. See Chesney-Lind and Paramore, "Gender and Gang Membership."

6. There is a growing body of literature that supports the link between childhood maltreatment and youths' subsequent involvement in delinquency. See Smith and Thornberry, "The Relationship between Childhood Maltreatment and Adolescent Involvement in Delinquency"; Widom, "Child Abuse, Neglect, and Violent Criminal Behavior."

7. See Bourgois and Dunlap, "Exorcising Sex-for-Crack"; Maher, *Sexed Work.*

8. Other research offers support for the relationship between girls' gang involvement and that of their family members. Moore's study of Chicano gang members in Los Angeles suggests that female gang members are often likely to have joined gangs because of a relative's association. In their interviews with gang members, Joe and Chesney-Lind report that 90 percent of the girls (twelve of thirteen) and 80 percent of the boys (twenty-eight of thirty-five) reported having a family member who was in a gang; usually this was a sibling. Although Lauderback and his colleagues argue that this pattern does not hold for African American females, whom they suggest are more likely to organize and join gangs independently, my research suggests that gang-involved family members are important contributors to African American girls' gang involvement. See Moore, *Going Down to the Barrio;* Joe and Chesney-Lind, "'Just Every Mother's Angel'"; Lauderback et al., "'Sisters Are Doin' It for Themselves.'"

   Geoffrey Hunt made an important observation about gangs and "family" during my presentation of a paper based on this study at the 1998 meetings of the American Sociological Association. While scholars typically talk about the gang as a "surrogate" family for young people, in fact there are many cases in which both "real" and "fictive" kin are members of girls' gangs. Thus, when young women speak of the familial nature of their gang relationships, they sometimes are literally speaking about their blood relatives.

9. See Collins, *Black Feminist Thought;* Hill, *The Strength of Black Families;* Scott and Black, "Deep Structures of African American Family Life"; Stack, *All Our Kin.*

10. Fortunately, when Dionne was interviewed for this project she was no longer living in her mother and uncle's home. She was living with her father, whom she described as "always giving her attention," and was in counseling to cope with what had happened to her.

References

Bjerregaard, Beth, and Carolyn Smith. 1993. "Gender Differences in Gang Participation, Delinquency, and Substance Use." *Journal of Quantitative Criminology* 4:329–355.

Bourgois, Philippe, and Eloise Dunlap. 1993. "Exorcising Sex-for-Crack: An Ethnographic Perspective from Harlem." In *Crack Pipe as Pimp: An Ethnographic Investigation of Sex-for-Crack Exchanges*, edited by Mitchell S. Ratner. New York: Lexington Books, pp. 97–132.

Canter, Rachelle J. 1982. "Family Correlates of Male and Female Delinquency." *Criminology* 20:149–167.

Cernkovich, S.A., and Peggy C. Giordano. 1987. "Family Relationships and Delinquency." *Criminology* 25:295–319.

Chesney-Lind, Meda, and Vickie V. Paramore. 1997. "Gender and Gang Membership: Exploring Youthful Motivations to Join Gangs." Paper presented at the Annual Meeting of the American Society of Criminology, San Diego.

Collins, Patricia Hill. 1990. *Black Feminist Thought: Knowledge, Consciousness, and the Politics of Empowerment*. Boston: Unwin Hyman.

Decker, Scott H., and Barrik Van Winkle. 1996. *Life in the Gang*. Cambridge, England: Cambridge University Press.

Esbensen, Finn-Aage, and Elizabeth Piper Deschenes. 1998. "A Multi-Site Examination of Gang Membership: Does Gender Matter?" *Criminology* 36:799–828.

Fleisher, Mark S. 1998. *Dead End Kids: Gang Girls and the Boys They Know*. Madison: Wisconsin University Press.

Hagan, John, A.R. Gillis, and John Simpson. 1985. "The Class Structure of Gender and Delinquency: Toward a Power-Control Theory of Common Delinquent Behavior." *American Journal of Sociology* 90:1151–1178.

Hagan, John, John Simpson, and A.R. Gillis. 1987. "Class in the Household: A Power-Control Theory of Gender and Delinquency." *American Journal of Sociology* 92:788–816.

Huff, C. Ronald. 1933. "Gangs in the United States." In *The Gang Intervention Handbook*, edited by Arnold P. Goldstein and C. Ronald Huff. Champaign, IL: Reserach Press, pp. 3–20.

Joe, Karen A., and Meda Chesney-Lind. 1995. "'Just Every Mother's Angel': An Analysis of Gender and Ethnic Variations in Youth Gang Membership." *Gender & Society* 9:408–430.

Lauderback, David, Joy Hansen, and Dan Waldorf. 1992. "'Sisters Are Doin' It for Themselves': A Black Female Gang in San Francisco." *The Gang Journal* 1:57–70.

Maher, Lisa. 1997. *Sexed Work: Gender, Race and Resistance in a Brooklyn Drug Market*. Oxford: Clarendon Press.

Moore, Joan. 1991. *Going Down to the Barrio: Homeboys and Homegirls in Change.* Philadelphia: Temple University Press.

Scott, Joseph W., and Albert Black. 1989. "Deep Structures of African American Family Life: Female and Male Kin Networks." *Western Journal of Black Studies* 13:17–24.

Singer, Simon I., and Murray Levine. 1988. "Power-Control Theory, Gender, and Delinquency: A Partial Replication with Additional Evidence on the Effects of Peers." *Criminology* 26:627–647.

Smith, Carolyn, and Terence P. Thornberry. 1995. "The Relationship Between Childhood Maltreatment and Adolescent Involvement in Delinquency." *Criminology* 33:451–479.

Smith, Douglas A., and Raymond Paternoster. 1987. "The Gender Gap in Theories of Deviance: Issues and Evidence." *Journal of Research in Crime and Delinquency* 24:140–172.

Stack, Carol. 1974. *All Our Kin: Strategies for Survival in a Black Community.* New York: Harper & Row.

Widom, Cathy Spatz. 1989. "Child Abuse, Neglect, and Violent Criminal Behavior." *Criminology* 27:251–271.

5

Asian Youths Join Gangs Because They Feel Culturally Alienated

Patrick Du Phuoc Long with Laura Ricard

Patrick Du Phuoc Long is a counselor to Indochinese children in juvenile correctional and rehabilitation facilities in California. Laura Ricard is coauthor of The Dream Shattered: Vietnamese Gangs in America.

Asian immigrants sometimes have a difficult time assimilating into American society. Some immigrant children are placed in classes that are too advanced for them; embarrassed and humiliated at their failure to understand their lessons, they start to skip school to hang out with gang members on the streets. Other Asian teens feel that they do not belong and are not accepted or understood by their parents or American society. The only place they feel a sense of belonging is in a gang with other alienated Asian youth.

Until South Vietnam fell to communist rule, all children attended school. Under communist rule, however, the children of South Vietnamese government officials and the offspring of American military personnel and government officials were not permitted to go, and children in these circumstances who made their way to the United States had little or no education. Nevertheless, when they arrived here they were plunged into schools with virtually no orientation, no preparation, and often no English. An enormous gap yawned between their skills and the demands of the classroom. Furthermore, children who had had some schooling in Vietnam quickly discovered that the American school setting was entirely different. In Vietnam, they played a passive role in class, listening politely and never questioning or challenging anything the teacher said. In American classrooms the system encourages, even demands, that students question their teachers. The new environment felt so alien and strange that these young people were confused, uncertain, and anxious.

Having come from Southeast Asian refugee camps, where for two to three years they received little if any education at all, most Indochinese children lagged several years behind other students their age. "I'm lost," a Cambodian girl said to me. Her mother is struggling to make her own living and is trying hard to learn English. But many parents like her do not know how to help their children stay in school.

School problems are a major reason children run away from home. A child struggling in the classroom and receiving nothing but criticism at home because of poor academic performance is likely to become truant. Having learned through friends where the coffee shops, skating rinks, and bowling alleys are, he begins to "hang out"—compared to school, these places are fun and exciting. As he misses more and more class time he sinks deeper and deeper into academic trouble. Eventually he gives up hope of accomplishing anything. Running away from his problems, he joins a gang and lives on the street. A Vietnamese juvenile serving at a correctional facility confessed:

> When I first set foot in America . . . I knew nothing about runaway and gang life. Schooling was my only pleasure in Vietnam, and [in the United States] I knew only school and homework [and] I had no idea of where to go for fun. Then, before long, I made many new friends at school. They knew where to go, such as coffee shops, skating rinks, bowling alleys, and parties. Once I got acquainted with these places I saw the differences between these places and my school. More and more I wanted to go out and felt bored at school. I kept losing interest in my studies and counted every minute for the school day to be over. Eventually I dropped out and before long, I joined a gang. My purpose was to enjoy going from one place to another to have a good time and also to avoid gang fights. These I fear. Confrontations with other gangs [occur] in the coffee shops, with provocative attitudes and verbal abuses. Fistfights happen. Then those who were beaten come back with guns to settle accounts.

To an extent the schools are to blame. More often than not administrators place children with no thought to their English language proficiency. Many children who were high achievers in Vietnam have failed here, and failure in school drives too many of these youngsters into gangs. Embarrassed, humiliated, lacking self-esteem and self-confidence, students on the edge of failure begin cutting classes. Then they become truant and drop out.

Recent arrivals who are deprived of effective guidance and tutorial assistance quickly give up when they are placed according to age and not language ability. They simply do not understand what is being taught in class. Consider the following examples of Vietnamese students who failed as a result of being placed in grade levels beyond their abilities:

Improper placement in class

Examples of Improper Placement of Refugee Children
    Le: Admitted to grade 9; assessed levels:
        Reading   grade 1

Vocabulary   grade 2
Math   grade 7
Mai: Admitted to grade 11; assessed levels:
Reading   grade 1
Vocabulary   grade 3
Math   grade 7
Dan: Admitted to grade 11; assessed levels:
Reading   grade 0
Vocabulary   grade 0
Math   grade 6

There are thousands of students like Le, Mai, and Dan who are admitted to classes that so exceed their abilities in English that they are destined to fail. The failure (or unwillingness) on the part of our schools to provide academic assistance in a variety of forms to these young people will drive them out of school and into gangs. As society will pay for this in the long run, it is certainly worth investing in their young lives now. In most schools, however, these kids are left to swim upstream on their own.[1]

Indochinese schoolchildren need more thoughtful attention from school placement officials and should be provided with remedial tutoring services. At home they need quiet places of their own to do homework, to read, and to study. "I have to use a coffee table, the floor, or the family kitchen, and my brothers and sisters are listening to music and watching Kung Fu videos," one of my wards reported. "I can't concentrate on my homework." Studying under these circumstances can be impossible. I have heard youngsters say that they just give up and leave the house.

Failure at school is often the beginning of the road to membership in gangs.

Parents must do everything they can to encourage the child to study, because failure at school is often the beginning of the road to membership in gangs. The sad fact is, however, that many Vietnamese have been forced to live in undesirable housing. They find themselves in run-down neighborhoods in cramped apartments that are simply not helpful to children who require a quiet space for study.

Thai's experiences illustrate the enormous difficulties faced by refugees struggling to make it in American schools. In summer 1988 Thai's parents put him aboard a fishing boat, expecting that the uncle who was with him would take good care of him. But the uncle was killed, and Thai found himself alone in a refugee camp in Indonesia. His sister had made her way to California, and she sponsored him. When he arrived in the United States Thai knew only the few words of English that he had picked up at the camp. Registering him for school, Thai's sister said he was one year younger than he was. In fact Thai was sixteen and two years older than his peers in grade nine. Thai's sister could not afford tutoring for him, so he rapidly began to fail most of his classes. He grew increasingly frustrated.

He began to cut classes. Then he quit going to school altogether, pretending to set off for classes in the morning so his sister would not question him. When school authorities notified her, she humiliated Thai by comparing him to the successful children of her friends and neighbors. Ultimately Thai ran away, joining other children of the streets. It was not long before he began to use drugs and to find a "home" with the Golden Eagles. Today Thai is a full-fledged member of one of San Jose's most notorious gangs.

Estrangement from American culture

Question: Do you consider yourself an American?

Answer: No!

Question: Do you consider yourself an Asian?

Answer: No! Everybody treats us like we don't belong here. And nobody seems to understand that we are a mixture. Cambodian, Filipino, Vietnamese.

Question: Are you a member of a gang?

Answer: I am and I'm proud of it [applause].

Question: Why did you join a gang?

Answer: Everybody looks at us as "other." Our parents don't understand us. So where do we feel like we belong? With our friends [loud applause].

Question: There are risks. Didn't you have alternatives?

Answer: Parents don't understand us. The world doesn't understand our parents. Everybody else seems to get attention. Nobody pays attention but our friends. No, there were no alternatives.

Question: Is it easy to join a gang?

Answer: To step in is easy. But to step out, your whole family can be killed.

This interview of a Santa Clara County juvenile reveals two important facts: first, that children need to belong, and second, that teenage Vietnamese gang members feel that society is indifferent to them. That angers them. Uncomfortable at home with parents who are "old-fashioned" and unable to make it in school, children like this gang member hate the law and despise society. Some actually take perverse pride in the fact that they lack the skills and education to live honestly. "I no read and I no write," one ward said to me, "but I can have anything I want—car, jewelry, beautiful girl."[2]

These children are lonely, bitterly disappointed in life, and, as the following poem suggests, longing for attention from their families (the first lines are like a refrain; I hear them over and over):

> Disappointed in my family, I ran away,
> Disappointed in my girlfriend, I joined the gang;
>
> Only now I have realized
> That the vagrants' law is killing me.
> When I leave, nobody sees me off,
> When I come home, I will be carried
> By six or seven pallbearers.
>
> Because of society, I did break-ins.
> Disappointed in my family, I ran away.

Many of these children bear tattoos on their wrists or arms that say *"Han Doi,"* or simply the initials "H.D.", or the word *"Han."* Each means "Resenting Society." Other tattoos that reflect their isolation and pain are *"Doi la So Khong"* (Life Is a Zero); "Tuoi Tre *Thieu Tinh Thuong"* (Youth Lacks Love); or *"Buon vi So Phan"* (I Feel Bad about My Destiny). These marks, often in the form of cigarette burns, are distressingly common on the bodies of the juvenile offenders I counsel.

Teenage Vietnamese gang members feel that society is indifferent to them.

Whatever the reasons, the juvenile members of gangs are not being integrated into American society. As one horrified Vietnamese observed in the aftermath of the Good Guys electronics store killings, "If the sons of [a respected member of the community] could do such a thing, it shows how far many Southeast Asian refugees are from being accepted into the American mainstream." In a similar vein a Vietnamese grocery store manager noted, "The younger people never saw anything good about Vietnam. . . . Because of the[ir] language problems and other things, they don't see much good here either. . . . The bad ones have many reasons to be bad."[3]

A world of their own

They create a world of their own in the gang. The surrogate family of the gang offers comradeship, understanding, respect, and approval. The world of street gangs is replete with its own rules, vocabularies, dress codes, tattoos, resources, and insignias. Gang names reflect the extent of members' estrangement and their inclination to violence and cruelty. I have identified 231 Indochinese gangs in California, but even a brief list of them suggests how alienated they are from society:

Asian Bad Boys
Asian Kicking Asses
Born To Violence (BTV)

Brotherhood of Crime
Cambodian Boyz Club (CBC, or Cold Blooded Cambodians)
Cheap Boyz
Death on Arrival
Dirty Punkz (Female)
Fuck The World
Innocent Bitch Killers (IBK)
Lao Killer Boyz (LKB)
Lonely Boyz Only
Ninja Clan Assassins
Oriental Killers
Scar Boys
South Side Scissorz
Vietnamese Trouble Makers (VTM)

"Read our message!" these appellations seem to say; "See how hostile we are!" Older Vietnamese people who fled the homeland recall that "in Vietnam I could not afford to buy a chicken, and for any move I made I needed permission from the village chief." For their children, however, "freedom" has come to mean the license to do anything they want in order to get what they want. They join gangs because gang life holds out the promise of material benefits. And yet, so many of these children live without hope or dreams of any kind, for lurking in the background is the ever-present threat of jail and death. As one Vietnamese boy named Dien wrote:

> In this world, no vagrant can elude jail:
> It's no fun to be a vagrant.
> To be so called, you have got to sniff, to inhale . . .
> Tears of pain run down my cheeks
> Make my heart bleak
> And my life a rubbish.

A California high school student observed, "We have been treated like outsiders. We haven't been accepted by the American culture. Gangs allow us to identify with something." The five-dot tattoos burned into their arms with cigarettes say it all: they symbolize *Tien* (money), *Tinh* (sex), *Thuoc* (drugs), *Toi* (crime), and *Tu* (jail).[4]

Notes

1. From official assessments of wards who have performance problems in school.

2. Patrick Du Phuoc Long, "The Whys of Vietnamese Gangs," in "A Selection of Readings," Book II, 132.

3. "Hostage: Relative Questions Tactics," *Sacramento Bee*, April 8, 1991.

4. Carol Izumikawa, "Hitting Home: Why Asian Gangs Often Target Their Own Communities," *City on a Hill Press*, March 10, 1994.

6

Drug Trafficking Encourages Gang Behavior

Lewis Yablonsky

Lewis Yablonsky, professor emeritus of sociology and criminology at the University of California, Northridge, is the author of several books on crime and juvenile deliquency, including Gangsters: Fifty Years of Madness, Drugs, and Death on the Streets of America.

Gangs during the 1950s and 1960s were not heavily involved in drug trafficking. However, during the 1990s drugs became an important and lucrative business for gangs. As a result, gangs have become much more violent—and due to the easy availability of guns and semiautomatic weapons, much more lethal—than they once were. Gangs use violence to maintain control over their drug-selling territory and to settle business disputes, often killing their rivals in an effort to build up a reputation. Drugs and their gang-related violence are becoming America's biggest crime problem.

Atrocious violence is one way of "putting in work" and rising in the hierarchy of the contemporary gang. Another pattern of significant "work" for a gangster is involved with the commerce of drugs. The gangs I studied and hung out with in the 1950s in New York City had a different connection to drugs than contemporary gangs. In earlier gangs, drug addiction was a side note to the social narcotic of violence that pervaded gang behavior. Most gangsters between the 1950s and the 1980s were not involved in the commerce of drugs.

In the 1950s, heroin was the major drug of gangsters. Rather than consolidating the gang, as occurs in contemporary gangs involved in the drug trade, drug use tended to break up early violent gangs. Their main activity involved gangbanging for kicks, and some measure of camaraderie, and drugs interfered with the effective performance of these tasks.

In the 1950s gang period, I observed that when a gangster started using heroin, he tended to drop out of the gang since his involvement with heroin addiction was an all-consuming activity. Heroin addiction tends to be a loner activity that requires daily forays into the community to commit thefts, burglaries, and muggings for the purpose of supporting an expensive habit. Feeding a heroin habit was a full-time job and didn't allow much time for gangbanging. Several gangs I was researching and working with in the 1950s broke up because a number of the gang's core gangsters became heroin addicts.

The role of original gangsters

The contemporary gangster's role in the business of drug dealing is related to his status in the gang. The L.A. Crips, which incorporate a number of different subgroups or "sets," provide a typical example. In the Crips, the "OGs" (the designation for original gangsters or older gangsters) are usually the prime managers of the gang's commerce of drugs. According to data I acquired from the head of an FBI gang task force, some Crip OGs have a direct connection to importing drugs from South American suppliers. "Gs" (middle-range gangsters still earning their stripes and a reputation) and "Wannabees" (younger gang member recruits) put in work serving as "mules" (transporting drugs) or selling drugs on the streets directly to consumers.

The OGs, who administer the overall drug-dealing operation, seldom get their hands dirty with the direct violence often necessary to maintain control over a drug business territory. If a dispute arises over their drug business or territory with a rival, they will commission a "hit" (an act of violence and sometimes murder) on the violating rival. The hit is usually carried out by younger gangsters who want to put in some work to acquire a reputation and status in their gang.

In the past decade, OGs, who earn small fortunes from the drug trade, will seldom get involved in senseless, nonprofitable gangbanging. They do on occasion serve as advisors to lower-level Wannabees and Gs involved in emotionally motivated gangbanging and drive-by violence.

In the contemporary violent gang, in a pattern similar to one that existed in earlier gangs, gangsters involved in the drug trade who become addicted are often shunned or dropped by the gang's leaders because they find them unreliable in their lucrative business. As one OG dealer told me, "If a guy starts using too much of the product, he becomes a fuckup, and we can't count on him for anything." In another interview, an OG who had become hooked on crack-cocaine told me, "I really wanted to clean up, not that I didn't love crack, but because it interfered with my business."

Drug-related violence

There are two patterns of gang violence: one is senseless, nonprofitable gangbanging, fighting another gang over territory that no one owns; the other is related to the drug business. This new pattern involving drugs and gang violence is not exclusive to the West Coast. It has become a phenomenon in almost all cities, large and small, in the United States. A *New York Times* article succinctly described the problem:

> They are a new breed of criminal in New York City: young members of crack-peddling gangs who murder on a whim.

> And though police officials say they are confident the gangs can be uprooted by methods that have worked before, other law-enforcement experts and social scientists are less optimistic.[1]

Sterling Johnson, Jr., a New York City special narcotics prosecutor, states in the same article,

> These gangs are more violent than anything this city has ever experienced. Crack cocaine has spawned an allied industry of young hit men who kill for the slightest reasons. In 1958 it took only 11 homicides in an outbreak of gang mayhem with zip guns and knives to stun the city. Recently in northern Manhattan alone, over the last five years, drug gangs have been responsible for as many as 500 gang-related murders, and most of these murders remain unsolved.[2]

Dr. Charles Bahn, a professor of forensic psychology at the John Jay College of Criminal Justice, is among those who believe the drug-oriented violent gangs I have described will be harder to eliminate than their predecessors. Based on his study of more than fifty gang members who have been arrested for murder and other felonies, he concluded: "Previous youth gangs were usually larger and they had a quasi-family role for their members. In these new gangs the social aspect is subordinate to the illegal drug business. There are more of these gangs, they are more antisocial and more ruthless."[3]

This form of drug-related gang violence struck a new chord with an incident in Boston that may be a prelude to a pattern, which now exists with the Mafia in Italy and the drug cartels of Colombia, of murdering troublesome public officials. On September 25, 1995, a forty-two-year-old prosecutor for the Massachusetts attorney general's office, Paul McLaughlin, who was well-known for the prosecution of inner-city gangsters, was gunned down by a young assassin. As McLaughlin was getting into his car, a hooded teenager emerged from the evening shadows, shouted some angry words, and shot him point-blank through his forehead. The hooded killer, who escaped from the scene of the crime, was identified by a witness as a fifteen to sixteen-year-old black teenager. In fact, McLaughlin at the time was in the process of prosecuting several Boston drug gangs. A comment made by a fellow member of the attorney general's office was ominous, "This pattern of assassination of law-enforcement officers, characteristic of Colombian drug lords, has come to America."

Violence-for-profit drug gangs

In a way, these new "violence-for-profit" drug gangs make more sense than the violent activities of the senseless gangbanger. The dealing of crack-cocaine drugs is a most profitable enterprise. It creates reality-based "turf," or territorial disputes. The enforcement of a profitable street-drug control position involves a more logical brand of violence than the senseless gangbanging violence that has no apparent purpose.

In the summer of 1994, twenty-two gang murders mostly connected to territorial disputes over the drug trade occurred in Venice, California.

The murders that took place came close to home. My son, a probation officer who lived in Venice during this period, called me one morning at 3 A.M. to tell me that there was the dead body of a sixteen-year-old youth at his front gate. All of the six sons of the family who lived across the street were in the gang drug business. The dead youth came from this family.

In a way, these new "violence-for-profit" drug gangs make more sense than the violent activities of the senseless gangbanger. The dealing of crack-cocaine drugs is a most profitable enterprise.

This murder is only one example of a pattern of homicides that plagues Los Angeles and other cities in the United States. My research visits to South Central L.A. revealed for me the impact violent drug gangs have on the ambiance of a community. This area of L.A. could be the set for some B movie about the world after a nuclear apocalypse. The area has become a nightmare landscape inhabited by marauding thugs. Innocent citizens living in the area are held hostage in their home by the nightly violence, and innocent people out on the streets late at night too often wind up as victims. When darkness comes to the hoods of L.A., many law-abiding citizens cower behind locked doors. Shadowy groups of young men pad quietly down the alleyways while police cruisers glide through the streets and the clatter of helicopters fills the sky.

The chilling impact that the violent drug gangs have on a community is cogently presented in a *Los Angeles Times* article that depicts how warring gangs can terrorize a neighborhood:

> In the shadow of commercial high-rises, the residents of a block-long stretch of Shatto Place live with a fear more natural to a place like Sarajevo. Rarely do they let their children play in the street or socialize outside the aging brick buildings that line the short block between Wilshire and 7th Street. Many are afraid to go outside because they, too, live on a battlefront. The 600 block of Shatto Place is controlled by one powerful street gang, and a rival gang's territory is just a block away. All too often, their war over turf and drug profits rages just outside the residents' doorsteps. . . .
>
> Lately, the casualties have escalated. On a Friday evening two weeks ago two young men, one of them a juvenile, were shot to death on the block by rival gang members, and a third victim was murdered in a shooting two days later. The second shooting resulted in yet another death. "It seems like every other day, something happens," said a resident who has lived on the block for three years. Life on the block means being constantly on the alert. One 20-year-old man who grew up on the block and still lives there has developed a survival tactic. Whenever an unfamiliar car drives by, he gets ready to hit the ground. "If a car

passes, I just get low. My friend's father got caught in cross-fire a couple of years ago."[4]

A pattern that has taken hold in some violent drug gangs involves transporting their drug empires to other cities. Two cases in point are the L.A. Crips and the prison-based Mexican Mafia. An interview I had with Charles Parsons, the special agent in charge of the Los Angeles FBI office, and his director of a special task force on gangs revealed that the Crips often send representatives to other cities to enlarge their lucrative drug operations. In 1995 the L.A. FBI Special Task Force on Gangs arrested twenty-two Mexican Mafia gang members. Two of the gang leaders were in prison at the time. The FBI prosecuted these gangsters under the federal Rico statute, originally promulgated for prosecuting organized crime (RICO stands for "Racketeering Influenced and Corrupt Organizations").

The nation's biggest problem

In summary, in the 1990s many violent gangs in New York, Chicago, Miami, Dallas, Cincinnati, and Washington, D.C., have entered the illegal drug business. They are actively spreading drugs and violence to other cities all across the country. In Chicago, where gang membership is now in the thousands, after a lull in the 1970s, the infamous El Rukins gang is under active investigation for drug trafficking. In New York, police are struggling to contain the explosion of drug-related violence. A Miami-based gang called the Untouchables is pushing crack northward to Atlanta, Savannah, and other cities of the Southeast, where the group is known and feared as the Miami Boys. An investigative reports TV documentary on the drug trade shows in detail how gangs have brought drugs from Colombia into a small city like Tyler, Texas.

The gangs' entry into drug trafficking on a major scale may be creating the nation's biggest crime problem in decades.

The gangs' entry into drug trafficking on a major scale may be creating the nation's biggest crime problem in decades. Drug profits are soaring and so is the drug-related homicide rate in cities where the gangs are most entrenched. It is arguable, in fact, that the emergence of drug gangs from coast to coast is very similar to what occurred during the early years of Prohibition, when La Cosa Nostra consolidated its status as an underworld cartel by building on the profits of illicit alcohol.

Today's drug gangs are far more erratically violent than the organized crime of the Mafia or La Cosa Nostra. A Mafia hit was and is more coordinated and focused on solving a "business problem." The new drug gangs that are derived from the gangbanging traditional gang are wilder and more lethal. This random violence is partially related to the younger Wannabee motivation to put in work toward building a reputation and status.

The large increase in violence is also due, as indicated, to the extraordinary availability of military and paramilitary weapons. Because of inadequate gun control laws, law enforcement agencies are relatively help-less in controlling guns on the streets of our cities. Guns like Uzis, AK 47 assault rifles, and AR15 semiautomatics are frequently bought (some even legally in gun shops) by gangsters, who finance their high-tech arsenals with profits from the drug trade. In effect, over the past decade the gun-blasting drug wars dramatized by the *Miami Vice* TV show and in ex-ploitative "action" films are played out in reality on the streets of cities around the country by this new form of violent gang.

Notes

1. Selwyn Raab, "A New Breed of Criminal," *New York Times,* March 20, 1988.

2. Ibid.

3. Ibid.

4. "Warring Gangs Keep Residents Fearful," *Los Angeles Times*, July 16, 1995.

7

The Media Encourage Gang Behavior

Rick Landre, Mike Miller, and Dee Porter

Rick Landre is the senior police officer of the Lodi (California) Gang Task Force Unit. Mike Miller is an educator with the California Youth Authority. Dee Porter teaches journalism and leads gang prevention programs. They are the authors of Gangs: A Handbook for Community Awareness.

The media glorifies gang violence through television news coverage, gangster rap and racist music, books, magazine articles, movies, and advertising. Gang members and gang-related violence are often sensationalized and exploited by the media in order to boost viewership and circulation. Gangster rap—a form of hip-hop music—is usually filled with angry and derogatory lyrics that promote violence against women and rival gangsters. Media coverage of notorious rap stars glamorizes the gangsters' lifestyle of violence, drugs, arrests, and promiscuity. Books, television, movies, and periodical articles have introduced and promoted gang values and ideologies to the American public.

If it bleeds, then it leads.

In April 1992, 18-year-old Ronald Ray Howard killed State Trooper Bill Davidson when stopped for driving a stolen vehicle in Houston, Texas. Howard, a crack cocaine dealer, later attempted to blame the influence of gangster rap music and an unhappy childhood growing up in the inner city for the shooting. The jury found him guilty as charged and sentenced Howard to death by lethal injection. A juror stated that although music can have a strong effect, people are ultimately responsible for their actions.

The influence of street gangs on our daily lives is best exemplified by the appearance of stories or urban myths based on gang culture. Several of these stories appear in media periodically as factual, as part of a news story, or as a story in itself due to the need for official denial by local authorities. These stories are now being posted on the Internet as a part of an urban myth Web site that portrays them for what they truly are. Although several myths may have at one time or place been based in fact, most often they are now too distorted to take seriously.

An example of this type of urban myth being circulated is the rumor of gang initiation requiring the murder of the occupant of the first vehicle to flash their headlights at a gang initiate's car. An incident similar to this occurred in Stockton, California, when a woman driving through a shopping mall parking lot flashed her headlights out of courtesy at a car with dimmed headlights that contained members of a local street gang. The gang members took this as a challenge or show of disrespect and killed the woman. Most peculiar is that most of these urban myths involving street gangs concern membership initiation.

Media influence on society

The entertainment, news, and advertising media exercise a powerful influence on society, and they have played a major role in the public's growing awareness of street gangs. Since the 1970s, newspapers and national magazines have carried stories on youth street gang problems, and such attention has increased exponentially during the 1980s and 1990s. A 1988 shooting outside a Stockton, California, theater may have been a turning point in the national media attention given to street gangs. Patrons waiting to buy tickets outside the theater were caught in the line of fire when a gang member committed a drive-by shooting, targeting a member of a rival gang who was standing in line. The people in line were waiting to see the film *Colors*, one of the first hit films about gang life and violence.

In such cases, the film celebrities become intimately connected to the gangsters firing shots. Entertainment media merges with the news media, and a relationship is established. The entertainment celebrities are sought to promote themselves and other products through advertising. However, this type of association may also backfire for the celebrity, as in the case of actor Edward James Olmos. He revealed in 1993 that he was being targeted for death by the Mexican Mafia due to his realistic, unflattering portrayal of the organization in the film *American Me*. As a result, he moves on a restricted schedule and in the accompaniment of bodyguards.

Often, the public has a difficult time separating the celebrity's image of gangster violence from the reality. The difference between image and reality is even harder to grasp for young people growing up with a barrage of images and ideas that are contrary to accepted public values.

Many fear that the antisocial values promoted in various media have created skewed attitudes and expectations of behavior for the nation's youth. Because of the tremendous influence media exercises, there is a national outcry for greater responsibility in the media today.

News coverage

Media decisions are motivated by complex forces. Television news reporting is no longer just the factual presentation of events. Most news producers feel a certain amount of sensationalism is necessary to gain viewers. More viewers result in higher ratings and, thus, greater advertising fees, which produce more revenue for the station. The story is very much the same for newspapers and magazines who need to maintain a level of readership that will guarantee continued advertising. The non-profit Rocky Mountain Media Watch Group surveyed 50 newscasts in 29 different cities on the night of January 11, 1995, and found that crime, disasters, and war made up 53 percent of the stories, with a high of over 70 percent in some cities.

Gang activity is easily exploited by news organizations as an attention-getting story. Most often, responsible journalism has prevailed with stories designed to inform the public about gangs. Occasionally, some news organization fails to be responsible and attempts to manipulate stories for increased sales or television ratings.

The influence of street gangs on our daily lives is best exemplified by the appearance of stories or urban myths based on gang culture.

A case in point occurred on the February 16, 1993, front page of *USA Today,* when the newspaper ran a story about the potential violence after the Rodney King trial controversy. Under the headline "Sooner or later, justice will happen," was an attention-grabbing photo of five young black men brandishing weapons and giving the camera a mean stare. The true story was that these five young men were part of an effort to promote a "guns for jobs" program that was organized by the community activist and singer Cashears to create positive alternatives for inner city youth. The young men believed, as did Cashears, that the photograph would be used as part of an article about their attempt to start a "guns for jobs" program in the South Central Los Angeles community. Tom Bradley, then mayor of Los Angeles, and Representative Maxine Waters, whose district includes South Central Los Angeles, were outraged at the paper's inappropriate use of the incident to sensationalize violence.

Readers wrote letters to the paper and severely criticized the blatant exploitive nature of the photograph. *USA Today* ran an apologetic editorial about accuracy and attempted to explain the misplaced photo as a bureaucratic mistake.

Gangster rap

The music most often associated with street gangs is a form of hip-hop music commonly known as *gangster rap* or *gangsta rap.* The origin of rap can be traced to the east coast of the United States in the late 1970s. Artists appeared on street corners, in underground clubs, and anywhere else an appreciative audience could be found. Commercial recordings of rap artists were few and far between until 1979, when the Sugarhill Gang released an album called *Rapper's Delight,* marking the commercial emergence of rap.

Throughout the 1980s rap became more popular, moving quickly across the country. Groups using mild lyrics and themes gave way to groups whose hard angry raps were laced with profanity. The trend continued through the early nineties with few restrictions on the vulgarity of rap lyrics. As the image of the gangster rapper became more closely tied to rap, rap lyrics talked more about life in the inner city and the social conscience, or lack thereof, of the artist.

Despite gangster rap's popularity among youth, radio stations across the country have called the music "socially irresponsible" and have edited offending lyrics, limited play, or refused to play it at all. Such actions were the subject of many feature news stories in 1993. Protests by several groups against gangster rap's derogatory portrayal of women and blacks became national news. Despite these objections, the saga of gangster rap continues. The tragedy of this situation is the failure of rap artists and recording companies to responsibly address the influence that their music has on young listeners. In September 1995, as a public response to outcries about the negativity and violence espoused by gangster rap, Time Warner divested itself of Interscope Records, which distributed its rap artists' music.

Sales analysis indicates that gangster rap is popular among blacks, Asians, Hispanics, and whites. Fascination with the "gangsta" image is creating a cult following for the "gangsta rap" stars, who cultivate an image as drug dealing gang bangers because that is what their fans admire.

Art mirrors life

The death in March 1995 of rapper Easy-E, a former member of the early rap group NWA (Niggaz With Attitude), forged the connection between image and reality. Easy-E, whose real name was Eric Wright, was only 31 at the time of his death from AIDS. Wright was born and raised in Compton, California, a gang-infested area of the Los Angeles metropolitan area.

A former drug dealer, Wright was a member of a notorious Compton-based street gang and used his gang credentials to promote the authenticity of his music. Wright even bragged about having fathered seven children by six different women, part of his image as a ruthless womanizer.

The entertainment, news, and advertising media exercise a powerful influence on society.

By having lived the life he rapped about, Wright promoted an image as an authentic gangster rapper. He was not a "studio gangster," as fans have labeled many rappers. Wright and NWA had a big impact on rap culture with the release of their 1988 album, *Straight Outta Compton*. It depicted vividly the lifestyle of street gangs, with lyrics about drive-by shootings, drug dealing, and confrontations with police. Its depiction of violence helped to sell over 2 million copies of the album despite the lack of radio play due to graphic contents.

Wright's life and death supported the negative messages of gangster rap—to live life fast and hard before dying. By dying young, Wright's immortalization as a rap star was ensured among young hip-hop followers.

Several other rap stars have also demonstrated that their art mirrors their life. Dr. Dre, another product of the Compton, California, gang scene, has a police record that helps to promote his gangster persona. He lives as though adhering to his own lyrics—"Rat-a-tat and a tat like that/Never hesitate to put a nigga on his back." Even after achieving celebrity as a rapper, Dr. Dre beat a woman in a Los Angeles night club.

The ongoing saga of Calvin Broadus, known more popularly as Snoop Doggy Dogg, is another example. He's been arrested for possession and sale of cocaine, charged with a weapons violation, and linked to the murder of a rival gang member by his bodyguard. Broadus followers believe these incidents help legitimize his work. The incidents do not seem to have hurt the sales of his 1993 release *Doggy Style* and the 1994 album *Murder Was the Case*. Despite this popularity, Snoop Doggy Dogg said, "As far as my acting career, I want a role of an attorney. I don't want to be remembered as a gang member."

Tupac Shakur, another successful actor and rapper, is also known for his scrapes with the law. In 1993, he was arrested for allegedly being involved in the shooting of two Atlanta, Georgia, police officers. Within three weeks, while he was out on bail, he was again charged as an accomplice, along with two associates, to the forcible sodomy and sexual abuse of a woman in a New York City hotel, a crime for which he received a sentence of four and a half years. Although he was imprisoned at the time and unable to promote or make a video, Shakur's latest album release, *Me Against the World*, was *Billboard* magazine's number-one album for several weeks during March and April of 1995.

Gang activity is easily exploited by news organizations as an attention-getting story.

Shakur's short span of stardom came to a halt when he died on Friday the 13th of September 1996. Six days earlier Shakur was the victim of his image after being shot several times by unknown assailants while riding in the car of Marion "Suge" Knight, the president of Death Row Records. This undoubtedly would raise his gangster image to an even higher level of reality and sell more albums.

Another rap artist, Christopher Wallace, known as the Notorious B.I.G., a.k.a. Biggie Smalls, was gunned down in March 1997 by unknown assailants. Wallace was known as an East Coast–style rap artist in contrast to Tupac Shakur's West Coast style. Rumors began to fly about a feud between gangs on each coast of the United States being responsible for the deaths of both rappers. The truth, however, is probably that each was a victim of his own hyped image that he created for himself, and it just got out of control. Gangsta rap may have reached its peak as record sales have begun to slow for the genre. Even Dr. Dre has softened his image and is said to be going back to a rhythm-and-blues style of music.

Music recording companies have not been shy in attempting to exploit gang rivalries and interest in gang lifestyle. In 1993, Dangerous Records released an album titled *Bangin' on Wax*. Sixteen supposed members of various Blood and Crip gangs from the Los Angeles area who were amateur rappers were featured on the album. To enhance the mystic image of the rappers, their faces were covered by bandannas in the appropriate blue or red colors, and they were listed on the album only by their street monikers. The album's producers claim their intent was to bring rival groups together to show them their similarities. Such peaceful intentions, however, were not evidenced in the album's selections, with such titles as "I Killed Ya Dead Homies" and "Another Slob Bites the Dust." The album producers also attempted to claim community responsibility by donating a percentage of the album's profits to recreational facilities in Compton and South Central Los Angeles.

Music, as an influence on gang violence and image, is not limited to the black rap artists who have received the most media and public attention. Several bands popular with Skinheads and white racist groups do not get equivalent coverage and are therefore largely unknown to most people. The groups' albums are not carried by most music stores as a result of their limited appeal. Some such music is only available through bootleg tapes passed around at meetings of white hate groups. These groups, including Screwdriver and White Rider, may appear to the uninformed as two more malevolent heavy metal rock groups, but careful listening reveals lyrics as vulgar, racist, and violent as those of the gangster rappers.

Gangs portrayed in books

In 1991 Léon Bing, a journalist who had written cover stories about Los Angeles gang life for *L.A. Weekly* and *Harper's* magazines, wrote a book titled *Do or Die*. The book sold many copies, introducing many readers to the attitudes and behavior of South Central Los Angeles street gangs. It described the difficulty its young characters faced living in the urban war zone created by street gangs and their violence. Bing recorded the actions and statements of both Blood and Crip gang members in a factual, enlightening presentation.

[Gangster and rap star Eric] Wright's life and death supported the negative messages of gangster rap—to live a life fast and hard before dying.

Bing's book introduces readers to street gang "hero" Kody Scott, known on the streets as Monster Kody. Scott joined his street gang in 1975 at age 11, and despite several gunshot wounds has survived life on the streets. He served time in the security housing unit of the California State Prison at Pelican Bay and is known as a ruthless killer who admits to participating in drive-by shootings from the age of eleven. At age 13, he acquired his street name, Monster, based on a brutal beating that he inflicted upon a robbery victim.

Scott, despite his lack of formal education, has educated himself. His 1993 book, *Monster: The Autobiography of an L.A. Gang Member* has sold over 75,000 copies in both hardback and paperback versions, earning Scott at least $200,000 in royalties.

While in prison, Scott took on the guise of a revolutionary and continues to portray himself and those who follow his beliefs as soldiers who are fighting an unjust system. His book is laced with references to the revolutionary ideology he promotes in the attempt to create a new-found image of himself as a guerrilla fighter. His ideology has resulted in a name change to Sanyika Shakur. Scott has also become a member of the Republic of New Afrika, an organization that advocates the takeover of five former slave states as a new homeland for American blacks.

Gangs on television and in the movies

Television and films have been a very popular and influential medium for transmitting information about gangs. The weak portrayal of L.A. gang life in the 1988 film, *Colors,* preceded several better and more realistic film representations. The primary focus of these films has been the L.A. gang scene, resulting in a predominance of knowledge across the nation about Crips and Blood.

The 1992 film *American Me* told the story of the origins of the notorious California prison gangs La Nuestra Familia and the Mexican Mafia. Actor Edward James Olmos portrayed one of the founders of the Mexican Mafia who was killed by his own gang. Shortly after the film opened, two consultants for the film were killed in gang-style executions, and Olmos believed himself to be in danger. He hired bodyguards and changed his normal activities accordingly. Suspicions about the wrath of the gang were confirmed when Joe Morgan, the godfather of the Mexican Mafia, filed a lawsuit against Olmos. Morgan claims that his life story is portrayed in the film without his consent. As of this writing, Olmos continues to worry about a possible contract on his life.

The 1994 HBO documentary *Gang War: Bangin' in Little Rock* gave a fresh view of gangs outside of L.A. Its portrayal of black and white gangs in Little Rock, Arkansas, showed the national migration of gang activity and the influence of popular music and film in promoting youth gang culture.

The 1994 film *Mi Vida Loca* presented a different angle on gangs. Following the lives of several Hispanic female gang members from the Echo Park section of Los Angeles, the film presented the impact of gangs from a female perspective. Although not a commercial success, the film did try to promote some understanding of gangs without gratuitous violence to make its points.

Gangs in periodical publications and advertising

Gang lifestyles and values have been introduced to young people across the country through a variety of periodicals. Most music magazines today cover the hip-hop scene with interviews, articles, and news about the stars and their latest escapades. Such articles may be mild, but they often include profanity, as well as talk of gangs and tagging.

Several youth music magazines, such as *The Source* and *Street Beat,* contain pictures to accompany their articles, including specialized graffiti sections that credit the creators of the graffiti and have tips on graffiti art, as well as interviews with some of the top graffiti artists. They provide a far-reaching billboard for taggers to display their work and promote their reputations.

One of the most interesting gang-related periodicals is *Teen Angels Magazine.* Published since 1981, this magazine is aimed at young Hispanic youth involved in the California gang culture. The magazine combines Hispanic pride in heritage, anti-Japanese rhetoric, and patriotism with warnings of government conspiracies. Featuring letters, drawings, and pictures by young Hispanics, it covers a variety of themes including gangs, prison, religion, and love.

Teen Angels invites readers to submit items for publication along with payments to "guarantee" their publication. Any criticism by media or community leaders of the magazine's contents is met with cries of racism in the magazine's editorials, although a cursory check will find flagrant anti-Japanese comments throughout the magazine.

Teen Angels Magazine also sends mixed messages to readers by publishing pictures of babies in gang regalia next to pictures of a gang member's funeral. Stores have refused to carry the magazine, citing its promotion of antisocial values among young readers in articles and photos comparable to those found in racist white hate group publications.

The street gang image plays a significant role in advertising, too. Mervyns, a major family-oriented department store, advertised a new line of clothing, using a photograph of a young boy wearing his jeans low enough to show the top two inches of his underwear. The style followed the trend set by Marky Mark, a popular rapper known for showing his underwear.

Television and films have been a very popular and influential medium for transmitting information about gangs.

Numerous callers to the store's headquarters did not like the fact that the store made this style of dressing appear acceptable by using it in its advertisements. Store management apologized to irate callers and promised to monitor future advertising more carefully for subtle messages.

A 1993 Nintendo advertisement showed a line of young boys attempting to appear menacing while performing drill team moves. To the casual observer the ad did appear very provocative, as the young boys wearing the video-game guns looked like idealized gang members. This ad became known in the advertising world as one of the worst ads of the year, as a result of its violent undertones.

Gang terms are even creeping into computer software. One children's writing program, My Own Stories, uses an example of a group of kids who call themselves the Mall Posse because they hang out at a local mall. Although the program's publishers may not have intended to refer to gang violence, My Own Stories is just one example of the extent to which the language of the street gang has become acceptable to the mainstream.

Meanwhile, the image-conscious National Football League has questioned players who wear bandannas or do-rags on the sidelines during games. Owners brought the subject up at the league's annual meeting in 1995, fearing that the players appeared too gang-like and could be misconstrued by young viewers as endorsing gangs.

8

Prison Life Encourages Gang Behavior

Tiffany Danitz

Tiffany Danitz is a writer for Insight on the News *magazine.*

Incarcerating gang members does not prevent gang members from running their gangs from prison or establishing new gangs while in prison. Prison gangs are flourishing across the country and are highly organized—even more so than street gangs. Gang members who are released from prison are often more sophisticated and more dangerous than when they went in. Prison gangs are often formed to control contraband, such as cigarettes, or for protection from predatory inmates. Although the rise in prison gangs is disturbing, by monitoring prison gangs, law enforcement authorities are becoming more knowledgeable about street gangs.

A 40-year-old gang leader uses his cellular phone to organize an elaborate drug ring and order hits. He commands respect. He wears gangbanger clothing and drapes himself with gold chains. This man is responsible for an entire network of gang members across the state of Illinois. He is Gino Colon, the mastermind behind the Latin Kings. When prosecutors finally caught up with him, Colon was indicted for running the Latin Kings' drug-dealing operation from behind prison walls—the state penitentiary in Menard.

"People in society and correctional officers need to understand that immediate control over the prison system is often an illusion at any time," says Cory Godwin, president of the gang-investigators association for the Florida Department of Corrections, or DC. "Contraband equals power."

Prison gangs are flourishing

Prison gangs are flourishing from California to Massachusetts. In 1996, the Federal Bureau of Prisons found that prison disturbances soared by about 400 percent in the early nineties, which authorities say indicated that gangs were becoming more active. In states such as Illinois, as much as 60 percent of the prison population belong to gangs, Godwin says. The Florida DC has identified 240 street gangs operating in their prisons. Street gangs, as opposed to gangs originating in prisons, are emerging as a larger problem on the East Coast.

Of the 143,000 inmates Texas houses in state pens, 5,000 have been identified as gang members and another 10,000 are under suspicion. Texas prison-gang expert Sammy Buentello says the state's prisons are not infested with gangs, but those that have set up shop are highly organized. "They have a paramilitary type structure," he says. "A majority of the people that come in have had experience with street-gang membership and have been brought up in that environment accepting it as the norm. But some join for survival."

After James Byrd Jr. was dragged to death in Jasper last June [1998], rumors spread throughout Texas linking two of the suspected assailants to racially charged prison gangs. While authorities and inmates dismiss these rumors, the Jasper murder occurred only weeks after a San Antonio grand jury indicted 16 members of the Mexican Mafia, one of the state's largest and most lethal prison gangs, for ordering the deaths of five people in San Antonio from within prison walls.

Of the two kinds of gangs, prison gangs and street gangs, the prison gangs are better organized.

"As they are being released into the community on parole, these people are becoming involved in actions related to prison-gang business. Consequently, it is no longer just a corrections problem—it is also a community problem," Buentello tells *Insight*.

According to gang investigators, the gang leaders communicate orders through letters. Where mail is monitored they may use a code—for instance, making every 12th word of a seemingly benign letter significant. They use visits, they put messages into their artwork and in some states they use the telephone. "It is a misnomer that when you lock a gang member up they fall off to Calcutta. They continue their activity," Godwin emphasizes. "It has only been in the last five years that law enforcement has realized that what happens on the inside can affect what happens on the outside and vice versa."

Of the two kinds of gangs, prison gangs and street gangs, the prison gangs are better organized, according to gang investigators. They developed within the prison system in California, Texas and Illinois in the 1940s and are low-key, discreet—even stealthy. They monitor members and dictate how they behave and treat each other. A serious violation means death, say investigators.

The street gangs are more flagrant. "Their members are going into the prisons and realizing that one of the reasons they are in prison is that they kept such a high profile" making it easier for the police to catch them, says Buentello. "So, they are coming out more sophisticated and more dangerous because they aren't as easily detected. They also network and keep track of who is out and so forth."

According to gang investigators and prisoners, the prison gangs were formed for protection against predatory inmates, but racketeering, black markets and racism became factors.

Godwin says Texas should never have outlawed smoking in the prisons, adding cigarettes as trade-goods contraband to the prohibited list. "If you go back to the Civil War era, to Andersonville prison," Godwin says of the prisoner-of-war facility for Union soldiers, "you will see that the first thing that developed was a gang because someone had to control the contraband—that is power. I'm convinced that if you put three people on an island somewhere, two would clique up and become predatory against the other at some point."

But protection remains an important factor. When a new inmate enters the prison system he is challenged to a fight, according to a Texas state-pen prisoner. The outcome determines who can fight, who will be extorted for protection money and who will become a servant to other prisoners. Those who can't join a gang or afford to spend $5 a week in commissary items for protection are destined to be servants. Godwin explains: "The environment is set up so that when you put that many people with antisocial behavior and criminal history together, someone is going to be the predator and someone the prey, and that is reality."

The Texas inmate describes a system in which gangs often recruit like fraternities, targeting short-term inmates because they can help the gang—pay them back, so to speak—when they leave prison for the free world. Most of the groups thrive on lifelong membership, according to the Florida DC, with "blood in, blood out" oaths extending leadership and membership beyond the prison into the lucrative drug trade, extortion and pressure rackets.

Prison gangs operating in Texas and Florida include Neta, the Texas Syndicate, the Aztecs, the Mexican Mafia, the New Black Panthers, the Black Guerrilla Family, Mandingo Warriors, Aryan Brotherhood, La Nuestra Familia, the Aryan Circle and the White Knights. Some of these gangs have alliances, and some are mortal enemies. Many on this list originated in California over the decades, some of them (such as the Texas Syndicate) to protect members from the other gangs. In addition, street gangs such as the Crips and Bloods and traditional racial-hate groups such as the Ku Klux Klan also operate in the prisons.

Monitoring prison gangs

What prisoners may not realize is that because the gangs are monitored by prison authorities the law-enforcement community is becoming very sophisticated about the gangs. "Sixty percent of what we learn about what is going on in the city streets of Florida" is garnered in prison and not from observing the streets, says Godwin.

Prison officials say they concentrate on inmate behavior to identify gang members. They do not single out gang leaders to strike any deals because acknowledging the gang as anything other than a "security-threat group" gives them too much credibility. This has been a particular problem in Puerto Rico with the native and political Neta gang. Recognizing groups during the 1970s, in a system in which prisoners have the right to vote, has led to a tendency among politicians to award clemency to some inmates.

Officials in Texas have reacted most stringently to gang members.

They isolate and place them in lockdown status to discourage membership. Buentello says this approach has produced a dramatic decrease in violence. In 1984, 53 inmates were killed due to gang violence. After the new policy was implemented in 1985, homicides dropped to five and then continued to decline.

Godwin says Florida uses a closed-management system that only locks up prisoners for 23 hours, with further enforcement based on inmate behavior.

"The reality is they are going to be able to get away with doing things when we have only a handful of prison staff," Godwin cautions, adding that the system needs to increase the professionalism of the staff with pay raises and training. Many employees are recruited out of the same neighborhoods as the prisoners, he explains.

Linda Washburn of the Massachusetts Department of Corrections, a much smaller system than Texas or Florida, says her state handles prisoner gangs just like Florida. According to her, size doesn't matter when it comes to prison-gang problems because no one is immune to it. "This issue crosses so many lines in society and in the prisons that it requires us in law enforcement and criminal justice to unite and confront the issue together . . . as a team with one voice."

It isn't about bad guys killing bad guys. It's about drug dealers and racketeers profiting off the system. And Godwin warns that the direct effect on American neighborhoods is realized when the 16-year-old sent up for 25 years gets paroled and moves in next door.

Organizations to Contact

The editors have compiled the following list of organizations concerned with the issues debated in this book. The descriptions are derived from materials provided by the organizations. All have publications or information available for interested readers. The list was compiled on the date of publication of the present volume; names, addresses, phone and fax numbers, and e-mail addresses may change. Be aware that many organizations take several weeks or longer to respond to inquiries, so allow as much time as possible.

California Youth Authority Office of Prevention and Victim Services (OPVS)
Office of Prevention and Victim Services
California Youth Authority
4241 Williamsbourgh Dr., Suite 214, Sacramento, CA 95823
(916) 262-1392
e-mail: klowe@cya.ca.gov • website: www.cya.ca.gov/organization/opvs.html

The Office of Prevention and Victim Services coordinates a wide range of victims services and administers several programs, including the Gang Violence Reduction Programs (GVRP). OPVS staff serve as consultants to local delinquency prevention programs and provide staff support for the State Commission on Juvenile Justice, Crime, and Delinquency Prevention. Its publications include the monthly newsletter *CYA Today.*

Center for the Community Interest
114 E. 32nd St., Suite 604, New York, NY 10016
(212) 689-6080 • fax: (212) 689-6370
e-mail: mail@communityinterest.org • website: www.communityinterest.org

The Center for the Community Interest (CCI) is a national organization that speaks out on crime and quality-of-life issues. CCI supports policies that strike a balance between rights and responsibilities and defends those policies when demands for civil liberties are carried to unreasonable extremes. Publications include the backgrounder "Juvenile Curfews."

Center for the Study and Prevention of Violence (CSPV)
Institute of Behavioral Science, University of Colorado at Boulder
Campus Box 439, Boulder, CO 80309-0439
(303) 492-8465 • fax: (303) 443-3297
e-mail: cspv@colorado.edu • website: www.colorado.edu/cspv

The purpose of the Center for the Study and Prevention of Violence is to provide information and assistance to organizations that are dedicated to preventing violence, particularly youth violence. Its Information House serves as a clearinghouse on research on the causes and prevention of violence. CSPV also offers technical assistance to organizations that are developing or evaluating violence prevention programs. Its publications include the paper "Gangs and Adolescent Violence," and the fact sheets "Gangs and Youth Violence" and "Female Juvenile Violence."

Gang and Youth Crime Prevention Program (GYCPP)
Ministry of Attorney General, Community Justice Branch
207-815 Hornby St., Vancouver, BC, V6Z 2E6 Canada
(604) 660-2605 • hotline: (800) 680-4264 (British Columbia only)
fax: (604) 775-2674

This program works with government ministries, police, public agencies, community-based organizations, and youth in order to raise awareness, and reduce the incidence, of gang- and youth-related crime and violence. GYCPP maintains a youth violence directory, conducts community forums and school workshops, creates videos, and publishes a set of booklets on Canada's criminal justice system.

The Heritage Foundation
214 Massachusetts Ave. NE, Washington, DC 20002
(202) 546-4400 • fax: (202) 546-8328

The Heritage Foundation is a conservative public policy research institute. It advocates tougher sentences and the construction of more prisons as means to reduce crime. The foundation publishes papers, including "How State and Local Officials Can Combat Violent Juvenile Crime," and the quarterly journal *Policy Review*, which occasionally contains articles addressing juvenile crime.

Milton S. Eisenhower Foundation
1660 L St. NW, Suite 200, Washington, DC 20036
(202) 429-0440
website: www.eisenhowerfoundation.org

The foundation consists of individuals dedicated to reducing crime in inner-city neighborhoods through community programs. It believes that more federally funded programs such as Head Start and Job Corps would improve education and job opportunities for youths, thus reducing juvenile crime and violence. The foundation's publications include the reports "To Establish Justice, to Ensure Domestic Tranquility: A Thirty Year Update of the National Commission on the Causes and Prevention of Violence," and "Youth Investment and Police Mentoring," and the monthly newsletter *Challenges from Within*.

National Council on Crime and Delinquency (NCCD)
1970 Broadway, Suite 500, Oakland, CA 94612
(510) 208-0500 • fax: (510) 208-0511
e-mail: rjohnson@itis.com • website: www.nccd-crc.org

The NCCD is composed of corrections specialists and others interested in the juvenile justice system and the prevention of crime and delinquency. It advocates community-based treatment programs rather than imprisonment for delinquent youths. It opposes placing minors in adult jails and executing those who commit capital offenses before the age of eighteen. Publications include the quarterlies *Crime and Delinquency* and *Journal of Research in Crime and Delinquency* and the papers "The Impact of the Justice System on Serious, Violent, and Chronic Juvenile Offenders," and "Images and Reality: Juvenile Crime, Youth Violence, and Public Policy."

National Crime Prevention Council (NCPC)
1000 Connecticut Ave. NW, 13th Floor, Washington, DC 20036
(202) 466-6272 • fax: (202) 296-1356

NCPC provides training and technical assistance to groups and individuals interested in crime prevention. It advocates job training and recreation programs as means to reduce youth crime and violence. The council, which sponsors the Take a Bite Out of Crime campaign, publishes the books *Preventing Violence: Program Ideas and Examples* and *350 Tested Strategies to Prevent Crime*, the booklet "Making Children, Families, and Communities Safer from Violence," and the newsletter *Catalyst*, which is published ten times a year.

National Institute of Justice (NIJ)
810 Seventh St. NW, Washington, DC 20531
(202) 307-2942 • fax: (202) 307-6394
website: www.ojp.usdoj.gov/nij

NIJ is the primary federal sponsor of research on crime and its control. It sponsors research efforts through grants and contracts that are carried out by universities, private institutions, and state and local agencies. Its publications include "Comparing the Criminal Behavior of Youth Gangs and At-Risk Youths," "High School Youths, Weapons, and Violence: A National Survey," and "Youth Afterschool Programs and Law Enforcement."

National School Safety Center (NSSC)
141 Duesenberg Dr., Suite 11, Westlake Village, CA 91362
(805) 373-9977 • fax: (805) 373-9277
e-mail: info@nssc1.org • website: www.nssc1.org

Part of Pepperdine University, the center is a research organization that studies school crime and violence, including gang and hate crimes, and that provides technical assistance to local school systems. NSSC believes that teacher training is an effective way of reducing juvenile crime. It publishes the booklet *Gangs in Schools: Breaking Up Is Hard to Do*, the *School Safety Update* newsletter, published nine times a year, and the resource papers "Safe Schools Overview" and "Weapons in Schools."

National Youth Gang Center (NYGC)
Institute for Intergovernmental Research, PO Box 12729, Tallahassee, FL 32317
(850) 385-0600 • fax: (850) 386-5356
e-mail: nygc@iir.com • website: www.iir.com/nygc

The National Youth Gang Center was developed by the Office of Juvenile Justice and Delinquency Prevention (OJJDP) to collect, analyze, and distribute information on gangs and gang-related legislation, research, and programs. Publications include research articles and fact sheets on topics such as gang statistics in the Youth Gang Series, prevention, intervention, and suppression programs, gangs and drugs, and gangs in schools.

Office of Juvenile Justice and Delinquency Prevention (OJJDP)
810 Seventh St. NW, Washington, DC 20531
(202) 307-5911 • fax: (202) 307-2093
e-mail: askjj@ojp.usdoj.gov • website: http://ojjdp.ncjrs.org

As the primary federal agency charged with monitoring and improving the juvenile justice system, the OJJDP develops and funds programs on juvenile justice. Among its goals are the prevention and control of illegal drug use and serious crime by juveniles. Through its Juvenile Justice Clearinghouse, the OJJDP distributes fact sheets, the annual *Youth Gang Survey* and reports such as "Youth Gangs: An Overview" and "Gang Suppression and Intervention: Community Models."

Teens Against Gang Violence
2 Moody St., Dorchester, MA 02124
(617) 282-9659 • fax: (617) 282-9659
e-mail: teensagv@aol.com • website: www.tagv.org

Teens Against Gang Violence, or T.A.G.V., is a volunteer, community-based, teen peer leadership program. T.A.G.V. distinguishes between gangs that are nonviolent and those that participate in violence. Through presentations and workshops, the organization educates teens, parents, schools and community groups on violence, guns, and drug prevention.

Youth Crime Watch of America (YCWA)
9300 S. Dadeland Blvd., Suite 100, Miami, FL 33156
(305) 670-2409 • fax: (305) 670-3805
e-mail: ycwa@ycwa.org • website: www.ycwa.org

YCWA is a nonprofit, student-led organization that promotes crime and drug prevention programs in communities and schools throughout the United States. Member-students at the elementary and secondary level help raise others' awareness concerning alcohol and drug abuse, crime, gangs, guns, and the importance of staying in school. Strategies include organizing student assemblies and patrols, conducting workshops, and challenging students to become personally involved in preventing crime and violence. YCWA publishes the quarterly newsletter *National Newswatch* and the *Community Based Youth Crime Watch Program Handbook*.

Bibliography

Books

Curtis W. Branch and Paul Pedersen, eds.   *Adolescent Gangs: Old Issues, New Approaches.* Philadelphia: Brunner/Mazel, 1999.

Douglas Century   *Street Kingdom: Five Years Inside the Franklin Avenue Posse.* New York: Warner Books, 1999.

Meda Chesney-Lind and John M. Hagedorn, eds.   *Female Gangs in America: Essays on Girls, Gangs, and Gender.* Chicago: Lake View Press, 1999.

G. David Curry and Scott H. Decker   *Confronting Gangs: Crime and Community.* Los Angeles: Roxbury, 1998.

Mark S. Fleisher   *Dead End Kids: Gang Girls and the Boys They Know.* Madison: University of Wisconsin Press, 1998.

James Garbarino   *Lost Boys: Why Our Sons Turn Violent and How We Can Save Them.* New York: Free Press, 1999.

Gus Gedatus   *Gangs and Violence.* Mankato, MN: LifeMatters, 2000.

Arnold P. Goldstein and Donald W. Kodluboy   *Gangs in Schools: Signs, Symbols, and Solutions.* Champaign, IL: Research Press, 1998.

Arturo Hernandez   *Peace in the Streets: Breaking the Cycle of Gang Violence.* Washington, DC: Child Welfare League of America, 1998.

James C. Howell   *Juvenile Justice and Youth Violence.* Thousand Oaks, CA: Sage, 1997.

C. Ronald Huff, ed.   *Gangs in America.* Thousand Oaks, CA: Sage, 1999.

Lonnie Jackson   *Gangbusters: Strategies for Prevention and Intervention.* Lanham, MD: American Correctional Association, 1998.

George W. Knox   *An Introduction to Gangs.* Rev. and expanded 5th ed. Peotone, IL: New Chicago School Press, 2000.

Rick Landre, Mike Miller, and Dee Porter   *Gangs: A Handbook for Community Awareness.* New York: Facts On File, 1997.

G. Larry Mays, ed.   *Gangs and Gang Behavior.* Chicago: Nelson-Hall, 1997.

Jody Miller   *One of the Guys: Girls, Gangs, and Gender.* New York: Oxford University Press, 2001.

Maryann Miller   *Coping with Weapons and Violence at School and on Your Streets.* New York: Rosen Publishing, 1999.

Dennise Orlando-Morningstar	*Street Gangs*. Washington, DC: Federal Judicial Center, 1997.
Susan A. Phillips	*Wallbangin': Graffiti and Gangs in L.A.* Chicago: University of Chicago Press, 1999.
Joseph Rodríguez, Rubén Martínez, and Luis J. Rodríguez	*East Side Stories: Gang Life in East L.A.* New York: PowerHouse Books, 1998.
Steven L. Sachs	*Street Gang Awareness: A Resource Guide for Parents and Professionals*. Minneapolis: Fairview Press, 1997.
Eric C. Schneider	*Vampires, Dragons, and Egyptian Kings: Youth Gangs in Postwar New York*. Princeton, NJ: Princeton University Press, 1999.
Gini Sikes	*8 Ball Chicks: A Year in the Violent World of Girl Gangsters*. New York: Doubleday, 1997.
Al Valdez	*Gangs: A Guide to Understanding Street Gangs*. San Clemente, CA: Lawtech Publishing, 1997.
Valerie Wiener	*Winning the War Against Youth Gangs: A Guide for Teens, Families, and Communities*. Westport, CT: Greenwood Publishing, 1999.
Lewis Yablonsky	*Gangsters: Fifty Years of Madness, Drugs, and Death on the Streets of America*. New York: New York University Press, 1997.

Periodicals

Craig Aaron	"Menaces to Society," *In These Times*, December 13, 1998.
David C. Anderson	"When Should Kids Go to Jail?" *American Prospect*, May/June 1998.
Vince Beiser	"Boyz on the Rez," *New Republic*, July 10, 2000.
Leon Bing	"Homegirls," *Rolling Stone*, April 12, 2001.
George Brooks	"Let's Not Gang Up on Our Kids," *U.S. Catholic*, March 1997.
Angie Cannon	"Kids Just Say No to Violence," *U.S. News & World Report*, November 1, 1999.
Terry Carter	"Equality with a Vengeance," *ABA Journal*, November 1999.
Warren Cohen	"The Windy City's Tough Tack on Street Gangs," *U.S. News & World Report*, December 14, 1998.
Roger Conner	"Rights for Gangs, Handcuffs for Neighborhoods," *Responsive Community*, Fall 1998. Available from 714 Gelman Library, George Washington University, Washington, DC 20052.
Tiffany Danitz	"Keeping Kids Out of Gangs," *Insight on the News*, July 6–13, 1998. Available from 3600 New York Ave. NE, Washington, DC 20002.

Gary Delgado	"Warriors for Peace: Stopping Youth Violence with Barrios Unidos," *Colorlines*, Winter 1999.
Debra Dickerson	"Cease-Fire in Simple City," *U.S. News & World Report*, March 16, 1998.
Richard L. Dukes, Ruben O. Martinez, and Judith A. Stein	"Precursors and Consequences of Membership in Youth Gangs," *Youth and Society*, December 1997. Available from Sage Publications, 2455 Teller Rd., Thousand Oaks, CA 91320.
Catherine Edwards	"When Girl Power Goes Gangsta," *Insight on the News*, March 20, 2000.
Evan Gahr	"Towns Turn Teens into Pumpkins," *Insight on the News*, February 3, 1997.
Joseph L. Galloway and Bruce Selcraig	"Into the Heart of Darkness," *U.S. News & World Report*, March 8, 1999.
Ted Gest	"A Taxpayer's Guide to Crime and Punishment," *U.S. News & World Report*, April 21, 1997.
John Gibeaut	"Gangbusters," *ABA Journal*, January 1998.
Errol A. Henderson	"Black Nationalism and Rap Music," *Journal of Black Studies*, January 1996. Available from Sage Publications, 2455 Teller Rd., Thousand Oaks, CA 91320.
Margaret Hornblower	"Ending the Roundups," *Time*, June 21, 1999.
Ann Hulbert	"The Influence of Anxiety," *New Republic*, December 7, 1998.
Juvenile Justice Bulletin	"Program of Research on the Causes and Correlates of Delinquency," October 1998. Available from Juvenile Justice Clearinghouse, PO Box 6000, Rockville, MD 20849-6000.
Susan Roberta Katz	"Presumed Guilty: How Schools Criminalize Latin Youth," *Social Justice*, January 1997.
Randall Kennedy	"Guilty by Association," *American Prospect*, May/June 1997.
Karen A. Joe Laidler and Geoffrey Hunt	"Violence and Social Organization in Female Gangs," *Social Justice*, Winter 1997.
Toni Locy	"Like Mother, Like Daughter," *U.S. News & World Report*, October 4, 1999.
Steve Lopez	"The Mutant Brady Bunch," *Time*, August 30, 1999.
Timothy W. Maier	"Street Gangs Move to 'Burbs," *Insight on the News*, July 6–13, 1998.
Greg Michie	"A Teacher Reflects on Kids and Gangs: 'You Gotta Be Hard,'" *Rethinking Schools*, Winter 1997–1998.
Joan Moore and John Hagedorn	"Female Gangs: A Focus on Research," *Juvenile Justice Bulletin*, March 2001. Available from www.ncjrs.org/html/ojjdp/jjbul2001_3_3/contents.html.

Paul Palango   "Danger Signs: How One Teen Salvaged Her Life,"
                            Maclean's, December 8, 1997.

Mary E. Pattillo   "Sweet Mothers and Gangbangers," *Social Forces*, March
                            1998.

Peter L. Patton   "The Gangstas in Our Midst," *Urban Review*, March 1998.
                            Available from Human Sciences Press, 233 Spring St.,
                            New York, NY 10013-1578.

Colin Powell   "I Wasn't Left to Myself," *Newsweek*, April 27, 1998.

Luis J. Rodríguez   "Hearts and Hand," *Social Justice*, Winter 1997.

Daniel J. Sharfstein   "Gangbusters: Enjoining the Boys in the 'Hood," *Ameri-
                            can Prospect*, May/June 1997.

Maureen Sheridan   "A Trade in Criminals," *Maclean's*, February 17, 1997.

Nina Siegal   "Ganging Up on Civil Liberties," *Progressive*, October
                            1997.

Gini Sikes   "Girls in the Hood," *Teen*, March 1997.

Ron Stodghill II   "In the Line of Fire," *Time*, April 20, 1998.

Andrew P. Thomas   "From Gangs to God," *Wall Street Journal*, October 23,
                            1998.

Kevin M. Thompson   "Youth Maltreatment and Gang Involvement," *Journal of
and Rhonda   Interpersonal Violence*, June 1998. Available from Sage
Braaten Antrim   Publications, 2455 Teller Rd., Thousand Oaks, CA 91320.

Robert L. Woodson   "A D.C. Neighborhood's Hard-Won Peace," *Wall Street
                            Journal*, February 21, 1997.

Lening Zhang,   "Youth Gangs, Drug Use, and Delinquency," *Journal of
John W. Welte, and   Criminal Justice*, March/April 1999. Available from
William F. Wieczorek   Elsevier Science, 655 Avenue of the Americas, New York,
                            NY 10010-5107.

Index

89